THE
PSYCHO-CULTURAL
UNDERPINNINGS OF
EVERYDAY FASCISM

THE PSYCHO-CULTURAL UNDERPINNINGS OF EVERYDAY FASCISM

Dialogue as Resistance

MARCIA TIBURI

BLOOMSBURY ACADEMIC
LONDON • NEW YORK • OXFORD • NEW DELHI • SYDNEY

BLOOMSBURY ACADEMIC
Bloomsbury Publishing Plc
50 Bedford Square, London, WC1B 3DP, UK
1385 Broadway, New York, NY 10018, USA
29 Earlsfort Terrace, Dublin 2, Ireland

BLOOMSBURY, BLOOMSBURY ACADEMIC and the Diana logo are
trademarks of Bloomsbury Publishing Plc

First published in 2015 in Brazil as *Como conversar com um fascista*
by Marcia Tiburi
First published in Great Britain 2022

Copyright © Marcia Tiburi, 2022

Marcia Tiburi has asserted her right under the Copyright, Designs and Patents
Act, 1988, to be identified as Author of this work.

For legal purposes the Acknowledgments on p. xv constitute an
extension of this copyright page.

Cover design by Holly Bell

Bloomsbury Publishing Plc does not have any control over, or responsibility for,
any third-party websites referred to or in this book. All internet addresses given
in this book were correct at the time of going to press. The author and publisher
regret any inconvenience caused if addresses have changed or sites have ceased
to exist, but can accept no responsibility for any such changes.

A catalogue record for this book is available from the British Library.

A catalog record for this book is available from the Library of Congress.

ISBN: HB: 978-1-3501-6536-6
PB: 978-1-3501-6537-3
ePDF: 978-1-3501-6538-0
eBook: 978-1-3501-6539-7

Typeset by RefineCatch Limited, Bungay, Suffolk
Printed and bound in Great Britain

To find out more about our authors and books visit www.bloomsbury.com
and sign up for our newsletters.

CONTENTS

FOREWORD

Brazil is a country famous for its exuberant nature. The Amazon Forest loved by tourists, who are also attracted by the fun of fabulous popular festivals such as Carnival. There are those who get to know Brazil through soccer players who become rich playing on foreign teams. Others know Brazil as the most extensive country in Latin America, and only one where Portuguese is spoken. Today Brazil is known for its high levels of social inequality, for state, urban and police violence, for crimes of racism, femicide, and the record killing of LGBTQIA+ people. A country where the prison population is immense, where human rights are not respected and where, incredible as it may seem, a strange president has been elected due to the equally strange fascist wave that has swept the country.

All over the world Bolsonaro has become the only issue involving the country, transformed into hell since his election. Using a terrifying hate speech and many demonstrations of prejudice, Bolsonaro was elected in 2018 and, despite all the evil he has been causing to the people, remains in office. Many wonder how he came to be president of a country that was emerging as an increasingly important economy on a global scale. Many also wonder how it was even possible that he was democratically elected. Some believe there was election fraud, others believe in brainwashing. Political processes have reasons that reason itself does not know. We know that the election was abnormal. To choose authoritarianism, under the penalty of

imploding democracy as has happened in Brazil, was not a
rational act. To understand a little better the process that has brought
Bolsonaro to power, we need to examine basic aspects of Brazilian
history.

The history of Brazil begins in 1500 with the arrival of the
Portuguese. Today we talk about "invasion" and no longer about
"discovery" as it was taught in schools during the 21 years of military
dictatorship, from 1964 to 1985, when the indigenous peoples
inhabiting the territory began to be decimated, precisely following
the European invasion. Those who survived have always been the
targets of continuous state violence. At the time this book the
indigenous people were greatly affected by COVID-19 in the absence
of adequate public policies; they have suffered the consequences of
negationism transformed into a form of government by current
President Jair Bolsonaro. Mining has been liberated in important
preserved territories and the assassination of environmental activist
leaders is becoming more and more common. There are increasingly
uncontrolled levels of deforestation. Bolsonaro is a national problem
for Brazilians who yearn for democracy, but he is also a worldwide
problem for those with ecological and democratic concerns.

Bolsonaro is the result of an authoritarian political history that
many people in Brazil believed to be part of the past. He was elected
by bringing back speeches that were thought to be overcome long ago.
Bolsonaro represents an immense regression and decadence for those
who believe in progressive social, political and economic ideas. As an
internal colonizer, Bolsonaro awkwardly declared his love for Donald
Trump and saluted the American flag while, at the same time, he
debauched the dead by COVID-19 in his own country. It is evident

that the typical authoritarian submission of the fascists has as correspondent the authoritarian aggressiveness against those who think differently from them. Bolsonaro is the neo-fascist, precisely because he is the new colonizer who is carrying out the neoliberalization project in Brazil and Latin America. To say that Brazil has become a neoliberal laboratory is nothing new. It is the recolonization that returns as a kind of destiny to those countries on the periphery of capitalism.

Colonization in Brazil is an ongoing process. Having started with the Portuguese, it was followed during the nineteenth and twentieth centuries by the arrival of Germans and Italians, and is continued today with national and foreign neoliberals, who show no respect for the country. Labor rights are being destroyed; all institutions are dismantled while at the same time, conservative ideologies that seemed to be consigned to history are beginning to re-emerge. Slavery as part of colonization formally ended in 1888, but, as in the USA, remains a festering wound on the Brazilian psyche.

Nowadays racism is considered a felony in Brazil. The issue was hidden for a long time, but has re-emerged following the rise of Bolsonaro. The issues surrounding exploitation of workers, the hatred for the poor, for women, the physically handicapped, the LGBTQI+ population, advances daily in the country culture. The general climate is one of political polarization. President Bolsonaro urged the entire population to arm themselves for a civil war while the number of deaths by COVID-19 continues to grow.

In this context, one can ask: how has fascism returned so quickly, when less than ten years ago Brazilians were approving Dilma Rousseff's government? Well, fascism is a political technology and has more difficulty sustaining itself in societies with high democratic density. However, it fructifies in countries where democracy is sparse and has not been able to confront its authoritarian past.

Since the Proclamation of the Republic at the end of the 19th century, Brazil has several coups d'état. The most traumatic was the Military Coup of 1964, responsible for the assassination of an entire progressive generation. That coup implemented a regime of economic, moral, political and cultural corruption that has not been elaborated until now. Twenty years after the coup, in the 1983 and 1984, the people took to the streets in a movement called "Diretas Já", but only managed to elect its representatives by direct vote in 1989. In 1988 a new Constitution was approved, which should have remained in force until today, but is, in practice, suspended. In fact, the country today exists as a kind of state of exception in which the legislative, the judiciary, the media and even the current religious powers are in league with each other when it comes to disrespecting the Constitution.

Brazil was governed by right-wing parties until 2002, when Luís Ignácio Lula da Silva, a metallurgical syndicalist, who had been one of the main leaders of the *Diretas Já* movement, was elected President of the Republic by the Workers' Party, the largest party in Latin America. Brazil lived its best years from that moment on. Dilma Rousseff was succeeded Lula in 2010 and was re-elected in 2014. During her term, she had the highest approval ratings as president, even more than Lula himself.

Dilma Rousseff was impeached in 2016 accused of fiscal mismanagement, but these charges have since been disproved.

President Jair Bolsonaro continues to practice the same policies, yet these are not "crimes" by the press or the judiciary, but purely budget "tricks". Jair Bolsonaro has committed real crimes, such as neglect of the public health crisis, interference in the Federal Police and obstruction of justice, ideological falsehood and support for anti-democratic actions, but yet the Federal Justice does not turn against him institutionally. More than sixty impeachment requests have been sent to Congress and it is widely acknowledged that the charges against Bolsonaro are much more serious than those that led to the successful prosecution of Rousseff. It may seem surreal but corrupt politicians are free while she, who has committed no crime, has been deposed.

For Lula da Silva it was even worse. He was arrested and imprisoned for over a year without evidence, on the false charge of receiving an apartment as a bribe. This is one of the most bizarre chapters of the so-called "Car Wash Operation (Operação Lava Jato)" that began in 2014 lead by a judge who later became Minister of Justice in Bolsonaro's government. Lula's persecution was notorious. The apartment in question was a low-scale property on a lower-middle-class beach that Lula had visited once, with his now deceased wife, but was not interested in buying. What mattered to his persecutors was any kind of scandal involving Lula that would destroy his image and, above all, keep him away from the electoral process. At the time of writing, former president Lula da Silva has been cleared, the charges against him have been annulled and his lawyers are still fighting to show how he was subjected to the politics of "Lawfare", that is, that politics in which the law is used as a weapon. The former judge is being judged for his criminal acts under the Brazilian Constitution.

The goal of Car Wash Operation was to remove Lula da Silva from the 2018 to pave the way for a candidate on the right, whose representatives were outraged at losing the elections to in 2002. However, the right-wing candidates were apathetic and had already been defeated by Lula and Dilma's party in previous elections. Car Wash Operation was fundamental. It produced arrests without evidence, proceeding against the proper legal processes. Spectacular coercive conduct was televised making it clear that the judiciary was allied with media powers in the 2018 election. Under Brazilian law, judges and prosecutors are not allowed to take political action, but this was not respected. Sérgio Moro and other agents of justice have been disrespecting the Constitution without any kind of control by the higher courts.

Rousseff was re-elected in 2014, but the previous year had been one of fierce symbolic disputes, when the fall of her government appeared to be taking place. Similarly, the depositions of the presidents in Honduras in 2009 and Paraguay in 2012 were produced without legal bases, in completely irregular processes. The same happened with Dilma Rousseff. There was one more element in Brazil's case: popular mobilization, built from 2013 onwards in a curious way.

In July 2013 the population of the largest Brazilian cities took the streets in protest against an increase in the cost of public transport. Everything resembled the Arab Spring. At first the masses seemed to be driven only by a democratic ideal repressed by the police. After a few days, however, the extreme right started to dominate the streets, using social media to incite a mood of hatred against the government. Even the hegemonic media, who had first attacking the demonstrations, later defended them in a clear manipulation of the popular agenda.

At this point, Bolsonaro had been a deputy for the state of Rio de Janeiro for over two decades. In the National Congress he was not taken seriously. He was even considered a person with mental problems. His ascent to power began in 2013 when he started to appear on social media networks, riding the wave of hatred that has started to invade Brazil. Hate speeches were promoted both on television and on social media networks by the most diverse and important figures on the political and media scene and Bolsonaro became a kind of keynote speaker. On April 17, 2016, the day Dilma Rousseff's impeachment was voted in the chamber of deputies, he made an inflammatory speech praising the colonel who had been Dilma Rousseff's torturer during her imprisonment in the military dictatorship. On that day, it was clear that the Brazilian nation was shocked by the speeches of deputies, many of whom approved the impeachment on behalf of their families and God. It was a real freak show, stuffed with rudeness and stupidity. Bolsonaro became a kind of hero, the Ubu Rei of the grotesque theater.

From then on, Bolsonaro gained more visibility than ever before. He, who had been considered "a bad element" by the Brazilian armed forces, ended up becoming not only the candidate of the anti-democratic forces in Brazil, but also of those that seemed democratic but willing to defeat the left at all costs. Supported by right-wing and far-right parties—which encompass the economic elite, the judiciary, the hegemonic media, and the evangelical churches—a marketing "character" was created with the help of Steve Bannon. The "character" Bolsonaro won the elections using illicit mechanisms such as mass

messaging by applications like WhatsApp, whose content was Fake
News against his opponent. Bolsonaro did not participate in the public
debates involving the candidates, making many suspect that the
stabbing he suffered in a crowd early in the campaign was used as an
excuse to retreat from the debates.

Brazil has become anti-democratic. The hate market industry
continues to grow for the benefit of the armament industry, of the
militarization that is becoming fiercer every day, and of the civil war
that may arise from internal tensions. What I call fascism in Brazil is
this industry technologically turbinated and economically sponsored
by groups interested in commanding the state for its market purposes.
Meanwhile, the struggle to defeat fascism enters the scene. It begins
with a dialogue capable of producing awareness of the danger that
humanity is exposed to at this moment.

ACKNOWLEDGMENTS

This edition was made possible with the help of several people. I thank the generosity of Monique Roelofs, as well as our friends Carla Damião, and Susana de Castro. I also thank my Brazilian publisher Lívia Vianna, as well as Carolina Torres and Letícia Feres, for all their support. Heloísa Villela, Wendia Machado, Helena Fietz, Nalu Romano, Melissa Andrade and Teresa Ribeiro were very helpful in revising the English text. I have no words to thank Renata Ferreira for her revision. She has always been generously available to read and review what I write. Myriam Marques, Natália de Campos, warriors in the Defend Democracy in Brazil for all kinds of help, which allowed me to continue my work at awkward moments. I thank Júnia Barreto and Gerard Wormser for all your support during my stay in Paris.

I would like to thank Colleen Coalter for her immense consideration and kindness with my work.

I would also like to thank James Green, Jonathan Warren, Eduardo Silva, Amy Chazkel, Conor Foley, João Nemi, who have always been very supportive of my books. To Eric Becker, I owe immense gratitude because he translated some extracts from the old Brazilian edition published in *Sampsonia Way* magazine edited by Tim Maddocks, to whom I also thank for always reviewing my texts and then making it much better. I also thank Magdalena Edwards and Idra Novey, who do not forget what I write. Thanks too to the friends of the City of

Asylum under the coordination of Abby Lembersky. With special thanks to Henry Reese and Diane Samuels for the wonderful housing in the hard winter of 2019 that gave me time to develop so many new projects at a time of great distress. I thank dear Cindy Nichols and her family for her attention to everything I write. I am very grateful to Jean Wyllys for always defending my book.

I also thank the University Paris 8 and the Programme Pause, in particular Sophie Wauquier, Diogo Sardinha and Soko Phay, as well as the Artist Protection Fund of the IIE (Institut of International Education) for supporting my research in visual arts and philosophy. I thank Rubens Casara, who helped me to give birth to this book, always with love.

I also thank my daughter, Maria Luiza who during the time of pandemic, has been around to support my tireless hours of writing.

Introduction

The Fascist Rise in Brazil

Ideological, codified elements, symbolic and aesthetic constructions allowed the advancement of an ordinary and maniac type such as Bolsonaro in Brazilian political culture, culminating with his seizure of power at the governmental level in 2018.

The first aspect to be analyzed to understand this phenomenon refers precisely to the concept of fascism applicable to the Bolsonaro case and to what has been generally called "bolsonarism". The second refers to the capitalization of the grotesque, the ridiculous, and the sexism in performances involving symbolic and decorative violence. Third, we must address the issue of disinformation raised to a paradigm in the context of the games of psycho-power that dominated the Brazilian mentality at the time of its fascistization. Finally, some considerations on fascism in the Brazilian context, neoliberalism, and the pandemic may help us to shed light on the darkness that covers us in this historical moment.

The term fascism, employed by Mussolini,[1] has been used in an expanded way for some time. In Brazil, potential fascism,[2] whose core is hatred against what is different, began to show more concrete signs in 2013, when the "June marchs" were manipulated by the media in favor of the Coup. Fascism is always an ideology and a political technology that is established in daily life by diverse movements, reaching psychosocially, individuals and groups. This ideology can advance through governments and states, producing death and mass destruction, as happened in Europe in the twentieth century and as it is happening in several countries of the world today. Above all, it is advancing, in this historical moment in Brazil.

We can define as fascism the phenomenon involving the rise of Jair Bolsonaro. Fascism is not only a characteristic of the current Brazilian government, made famous for its promotion of barbarity against women, indigenous people, quilombola[3] people, LGBTQI+, left-wing parties and democracy. It also includes the construction that led to its rise, as well as the forces that sustain it today. Fascism today is, therefore, the process by which democracy entered a state of exception, presenting itself as a empty signifier[4] of an authoritarian regime involving the judiciary, the legislative power, the media, and some religious groups. Fascism is the project of destruction of Brazil within the scope of neoliberalism.[5]

---

[1] Paxton, Robert Owe. *Anatomy of Fascism*. London: Penguin, 2004.

[2] Adorno, Theodor; Frenkel-Brunswik, Else; Levinson, Daniel; Sanford, Nevitt. *The Authoritarian Personality*. London and New York: Verso, 2019.

[3] Afro-descendants who live in places called "quilombos" (War camp in Kimbundu). The quilombos were founded by ancestors who rebelled against the slavery system.

[4] Laclau, Ernesto. *Emancipação e Diferença*. Rio de Janeiro : EDUERJ, 2011.

[5] Ianni, Octavio. "Neoliberalismo e Nazi-fascismo." *Crítica Marxista*, São Paulo, Shaman, Vol.1, No. 7, 1998, pp. 112–20.

Fascism is the appropriate name to speak about the right-wing extremists that returned from the underground of history to our days. It sums up the dominant authoritarian tendency articulated as technology or the methodology of mass enchantment. Bolsonaro became the oligarchies' puppet. Despite managing economic, media and religious power in Brazil, the right-wing oligarchs didn't have strong candidates to overthrow the left. They used him in the election of 2018 for his popular charisma among conservatives. We can say that Bolsonaro is the legitimate representative of "voodoo"[6] politics and economics, the "crazy man"[7] able to do everything in the name of power, who is, at the same time, used to turn the Brazilian nation into a hypnotic frenzy. The manipulation is carried out by the extreme right, hides behind him.

Bolsonaro's performance opens up space for the neoliberal project of the destruction of the country. Bolsonaro is the façade of a project infinitely more difficult to overcome. The dismantling of the democratic state and the cancellation of fundamental rights advances without limits in the hands of the ministers of economy and environment (Paulo Guedes and João Salles), responsible for privatizations and the destruction of environmental protection's laws. Brazil resembles a colony from which cheap labor is demeaned and natural resources can be extracted as in old times.

The racist, misogynistic, ultra-conservative, military and dictatorial Brazilian oligarchies created the conditions for the rise of Bolsonaro. These oligarchies constitute the "bolsonarism," which includes the

---

[6] Harvey, David. *The Condition of Postmodernity*. Oxford: Blackwell, 1989.
[7] ADORNO, Theodor. *Aspekte des neuen Rechtsradikalismus*. Berlin: Suhrkamp, 2019.

current renegades; politicians who previously supported and collaborated with him. Today they try to differentiate themselves from him, even to become candidates in the next elections, as is the case of the former judge Sérgio Moro.[8] Even though Jair Bolsonaro attacks those who put him in power and displeases the upper bourgeoisie, who would prefer a more "aesthetically correct" person and even after he and his secretaries of state have committed crimes of responsibility, they all remain in office in the name of ongoing neoliberal domination.

As a matter of fact, as long as Bolsonaro is useful to the oligarchies, he will remain in power. In this line, fascism advances not only as a front or ideology that covers up neoliberalism, but also as a real industry and market. It is the cultural industry of fascism that is developing today under new historical and micro-technological conditions. Capital investments under fascism generate more capital, as well as digital speed increments and the technical transmissibility of content, imprinting a new intensity on the process of fascistization, with expected results arriving much faster.

We can define as "turbofascism" the digital[9] economic and technological intensification of fascism in our time. Unlike the fascists of the early twentieth century, today's fascists can make use of all kinds of digital technology to act much more efficiently, along with companies

---

[8] Sérgio Moro is the former judge who arrested Lula while committing countless illegalities. Raised the hero of the extreme right, he was awarded the position of Ministrer of Justice after election, but walked away from Bolsonaro in an attempt to remove right-wing parties from the management of the health crisis during the pandemic. In 2021 the Brazilian Supreme Court tried Lula's case and he was acquitted. The charges against him were false and were overturned. While I write this note, the judge is being tried by the Supreme Court.
[9] See the documentary *The Great Hack*, 2019, by Karim Amer and Jehane Noujaim.

and capital investors targeting the control of such technologies. Ideology increasingly becomes a technological and marketing issue. An industry and market is set up Facebook and so on by the far right, in which social networks, such as WhatsApp, are used to spread lies, smear campaigns and "Fake News."[10] Even elements that might seem purely ideological, such as hatred for the left, are turned into merchandise. Ideology is no longer just a veil that covers up market interests or false consciousness. It has become the very commodity that, in the form of hate speech and misinformation, has a high power to mobilize emotions using seemingly narcotic powers offered to the masses.

A true political economy of language, involving the production and consumption of hatred and misinformation, advances as a corporate fascist market in Brazil. The so-called "Office of Hate"[11] uses hate as a raw material, cultivating and distributing it with tailor-made prices to all classes. So, if McDonald's sells sandwiches with varied ingredients, the hate market sells misogyny, racism, xenophobia, capacitism, anti-intellectualism, cult and promise of return to the military dictatorship, subservience to the USA, end of human/civil rights, and the most diverse forms of prejudice. The target audience are those who have been devoid of political sense, the undecided,

---

[10] This type of activity is of course prohibited in Brazil, but the far right used it during the 2018 campaign via mobile phones with foreign numbers: https://www1.folha.uol.com.br/poder/2019/10/whatsapp-admite-envio-massivo-ilegal-de-mensagens-nas-eleicoes-de-2018.shtml. See also: https://www.uol.com.br/tilt/noticias/redacao/2020/07/02/proibidas-pela-justica-maquinas-de-spam-no-whatsapp-continuam-operando.htm

[11] Said, Flavia. "Ex-aliados de Bolsonaro mostram como funciona o Gabinete do Ódio" *Congresso em Foco*. Brasília, May 28, 2020. Available at: www.congressoemfoco.uol.com.br/governo/ex-aliados-de-bolsonaro-detalham-modus-operandi-do-gabinete-do-odio/

those who abstain, the political skeptic, the easy victims of advertising campaigns. The enemies of the neoliberal regime have also been reduced to a commodity. In this sense, Brazilian's leftists became at once the object of a political and economic investment: laborious attacks from conservative media that resulted in direct economic and monetary profit.[12] A policy of enmity[13] corresponds to an economy of hostility. Enmity becomes paradigmatic in fascist populism. At its base, managed paranoia is elevated to a form of government at war against institutions. It is aimed against universities, education as a whole, knowledge, science and the arts. Brazil's current government members defend flat earth and negationist conspiracy theories in order to influence masses into frenzy and confusion.

The new micro-technologies and especially the digital technology of the Internet have changed what we call fascism. The fascism of the twentieth century did not include television, which appeared in 1950, only after the end of the Second World War. Today's fascism relies on television, which in Brazil has been, for decades now, the daily source bombarding high doses of bias and misinformation, forming a kind of lazy citizen, prostrated before the screens.[14] The social networks only continue in an accelerated way this old work of desubjectivation.

---

[12] https://theintercept.com/2019/11/19/fake-news-google-blogueiros-antipetistas/

[13] Mbembe, Achille. *Políticas da Inimizade*. Trans. Maria Lança. Lisboa: Antigona, 2017.

[14] Tiburi, Marcia. Olho de Vidro. *A televisão e o estado de exceção da imagem* [*Glass eye: the television and the state of exception of the image*]. Rio de Janeiro: Record, 2011.

Grotesque Performance, Machismo and Cynicism

The "gun" gesture, used as a mark by Bolsonaro during his campaign in 2018, became less frequent since Brazilians have been calling him "genocidal." That gesture was like a symbolic "sweet" threat, a "cute" threat. Part of the bolsonarist fascist code, the threat transformed into an advertising trait, has conquered millions of people. In the sequence, one of Bolsonaro's first resolutions was to free up gun licences in Brazil. This political act involved the widespread authorization of war and the killing of people by the police. Today it is clear that the lack of public policies to confront the coronavirus pandemic is part of the project to let the vulnerable population die, in a direct attack on human rights.[15]

The violence we see from the government, whether verbal, symbolic, or physical, has an ostentatious function. The perceived threat is projected in the form of fear imposed to people. Fascism is the aesthetic of terrorist capitalism in its desperate phase. When the system perceives the threat overcoming it, it further intensifies its methods of producing hegemony. Fascist war implies hegemonic victory on a political and aesthetic level. Although the latter is generally neglected, if well analyzed it offers a map of the system of prejudices that aims at eliminating what and who is different.

---

[15] https://noticias.uol.com.br/ultimas-noticias/rfi/2020/07/01/mais-de-60-ongs-denunciam-governo-bolsonaro-na-onu-por-violacoes-de-direitos-humanos-na-pandemia.htm

In Brazil, a grotesque, infamous and ridiculous speech[16] allowed the fascist rise from the coup of 2016.[17] Bolsonaro became well known when he spoke in favor of torture on the day of the impeachment of President Dilma Rousseff. Besides Bolsonaro, the candidates, who in the 2018 election made use of a capitalization of the ridiculous at the absurd level, were the most voted. The grotesque discourse is political technology used as advertisement for violence. The decorative and ostentatious violence exhibited in the daily grotesque speeches of their representatives allows them notoriety and spectacular capital.

Scenes of aesthetic-political brutality are decisive in the capitalization of Bolsonaro and similar politicians. In their speeches, they invest in bad words and unpleasant scenes that portray them as capable of anger and rage. Bolsonaro acts as an hysterical male, screaming while holding a weapon; gestures that grant him the power to attack at any moment by renewing the sense of threat.

Decorative violence is on the rise in Brazilian and Latin American politics. If in Mexico, "gore capitalism"[18] plays to the aesthetics of the narcotrafficker, in Brazil the aesthetic is one of "militia," the male bearer of weapons. Jair Bolsonaro's sons usually appear in photos with guns. One of them even carried a gun to a demonstration on Avenida Paulista against the Worker's Party well before his father became president[19] and

---

[16] See Foucault, Michel. *Les Anormaux. Cours au Collège de France, 1974-1975*. Ehhess, Gallimard, Seuil, 1999.

[17] See Tiburi, Marcia. *Ridículo Político. O risível, manipulação da imagem e o esteticamente correto [Political ridiculous. The laughable, image manipulation and the aesthetically correct]*. Rio de Janeiro: Record, 2017.

[18] Sayak, Valencia Triana. "Capitalismo *gore* y necropolítica en México contemporâneo" [*Gore* and necropolitical capitalism in contemporary Mexico]. Relaciones Internacionales, No. 19, February 2012. GERI - UAM.

[19] https://piaui.folha.uol.com.br/materia/o-debutante/

also appeared armed in photos. In a moment of fervor for this aesthetic of violence, Sérgio Moro, then minister of justice, posed for a picture alongside a self-portrait made with bullet shells.[20]

The acts of decoration of military policemen and militiamen are also part of this aesthetic of spectacular violence used by Bolsonaro and his sons. The case of the decoration by, then state representative, Flávio Bolsonaro of a former policeman who later became the suspect in the murder of Marielle Franco,[21] became notorious. This policeman was honored in 2005 while serving time for murder and was himself murdered in 2019.[22] Flávio Bolsonaro spectacularly posted pictures of his corpse on social networks.[23] The ideology is aesthetic and works in managing the population's fear of meeting the same fate.

In this scenario, the far right has also been using sexuality as a weapon of war. In the carnival of 2019, Bolsonaro caused astonishment by posting on Twitter a video of a scene called a *golden shower*.[24] The explicit goal was to cause strangeness and dread. It was a calculated excess to destroy the Brazilian carnival with a moralistic speech and to

---

[20] www.noticias.uol.com.br/politica/ultimas-noticias/2019/12/11/moro-ganha-obra-de-cartuchos-de-bala.htm

[21] Marielle Franco was a young black councilwoman who was murdered, along with her driver, in March 2018. Two suspects were arrested and a third participant, who was in the car, is still missing. All investigations point to the third suspect being one of Bolsonaro's sons, but Bolsonaro has interfered in the police investigations about the case. The two prisoners were at Bolsonaro's house on the day of Marielle's murder. Seee www1.folha.uol.com.br/poder/2020/03/veja-tudo-o-que-sesabe-sobre-a-morte-de-marielle-dois-anos-depois.shtml

[22] www.brasil.elpais.com/brasil/2019-12-20/a-trajetoria-do-chefe-miliciano-que-recebia-parte-da-rachadinha-de-flavio-bolsonaro-segundo-o-mp.html

[23] https://jornaldebrasilia.com.br/politica-e-poder/video-flavio-bolsonaro-expoe-nas-redes-sociais-a-autopsia-de-capitao-adriano/

[24] Oliveira Júnior, Ribamar José. "Capitalismo Gore no Brasil: entre farmacopornografia e necropolítica, o golden shower e a continência de Bolsonaro". *Revista Sociologias Plurais*, Vol. 5, No. 1, pp. 245–72, July, 2019.

attack various sectors. Bolsonaro had to step back and delete the Tweet for crossing the limits of public decency. It was no different when two candidates for deputy from Rio de Janeiro broke a street sign bearing Marielle Franco's name during the 2018 campaign and got themselves elected with the vast majority of votes in a display of fascism in a pure state against the memory of a black and lesbian councilwoman, a human rights defender who had been murdered by militias that year.

Misogyny was the keynote in the advertising campaign used against Dilma Rousseff in the coup d'état process. The basic strategy of the hegemonic media was to associate her with madness, as a tactic that has historically been used against women. Before the 2016 coup, in a perversion of advertising, bumper stickers circulated showing Dilma's face glued to a female's body with open legs and, in the pubic area, a fuel pump nozzle turned into a substitute for a penis. It was the apology of rape that traveled through the streets, naturalizing the aesthetic of allegorical violence.

In the same line of allegory of sexual violence, several stories like Fake News were created as artifacts of creative refinement: the so-called "gay kit," which would be a teaching material to turn children into homosexuals, as well as a bottle with a beak in the shape of a penis. According to this spread of stories, the Workers' Party was distributing these objects in schools. It may seem preposterous, but, unfortunately, the underprivileged Brazilian population, hypnotized by fascism, believed these lies, as they are still encouraged to believe that "communists" eat little children. It is not by chance that the use of the term *pedophilia* is present all the time in government speeches, especially those of the minister of human rights and women, Damares Alves, herself an evangelical pastor, who plays an important role in Bolsonaro's government as one of the greatest exponents of the grotesque speeches relating to sex.

Psycho-Power

Just as Foucault defined biopower as the calculation that power does over life and "thanatopower" as the calculation that power does over death,[25] we can account for the calculation that power does over what people think and feel. It is a calculation about language, the ideological calculation par excellence. The ideological media produce their programming according to this calculation.

Throughout history, power has always calculated in view of the internal capacity of the population to perceive the manipulations against it, which would be the task of intellectuals in general, educators, teachers and artists. To destroy this natural front of resistance is a fundamental task of ideologies. Beyond the persecution, forged by the demonization of characters in the usual witch-hunt climate that yields important results, but does not conquer the totality of single thinking or the total domination to which the ideology aspires, a fatal weapon arises in relation to language procedures. It is cynicism that comes to replace the whole structure of language games which sustained the construction of the public sphere and political struggles for recognition and rights. Cynism not only interrupts the linguistic forms of democracy, but it also prevents the continuity of any order of

---

[25] Foucault, Michel. *Histoire de la Sexualité* [*History of sexuality*]. La Volonté de Savoir. Paris, Gallimard, 1994. See: Tiburi, Marcia. Delírio do Poder – psicopoder e loucura coletiva na era da desinformação, Record, 2019.

discourse. Cynicism is the death of language and, with it, the death of politics. The truth is a value sequestered by all ideologies, but in fascism it is simply destroyed. The destruction of truth gives way to a kind of cynical episteme in which misinformation is the new paradigm. The distorted, falsified, illusory information produces an environment in which all experience is given, from which everyone is subjected cognitively and emotionally and thus, led to act like robots. In this sense, politicians, media and churches have been producing spectacular and abject scenes with the objective of shocking the masses. Such scenes are ritual images capable of touching unprotected people in a subjective way, affecting perception. Shocked daily by false and violent information, reached in the "physiological" plan of their experiences,[26] people let themselves be carried away without any chance to exercise the critical and reflective thinking that, since Adorno and Horkheimer,[27] has been the main enemy of fascism which has rightly been destroyed by it.

Critical thinking is what cynicism aims to completely annihilate. Psycho-power is, in turn, the set of ways in which lies are implanted so that they can take the place of truth. It is not a simple lie that could be perceived by everyone or that, unmasked, would return us to the truth. It is a modification of the very meaning of the lie and truth in the construction of the cynical circle, the agreement between cynics and suckers to which, whoever is in disagreement is transformed into the enemy, persecuted and demonized.

---

[26] Türcke, Christoph. *Sociedade Excitada: filosofia da sensação* [*Excited society: Philosophy of sensation*]. Campinas: Unicamp, 2010.

[27] Adorno, Theodor Wisengrund and Horkheimer, Max. *Dialektik der Aufklärung. Philosophische Fragmente*. In: Adorno, Theodor Wisengrund. *Gesammelte Werke*, Vol. 3. Frankfurt am Main: Suhrkamp, 1997.

Whole populations are led to follow the authoritarian ideology through processes of psycho-power involving not only the traditional media and social networks, but also the churches of the market (the neo-Pentecostal evangelical churches), which spread prejudice and hate speech, but also religious violence, even against the Catholic Church, but above all, against religions of African origin.

In Brazil, neo-Pentecostal pastors of the so-called "market churches"[28] become wealthy using psycho-power techniques, taking advantage of the emotional and material frailties of the poorest population. Today, Brazilian politics is so linked to religion that it has become common for pastors to be elected to the National Congress. Bolsonaro's baptism[29] by one of these pastor-politicians was a ritual spectacle that marked his joint project with the neo-Pentecostal church. In addition, religious hatred walks *pari passu* with hatred of women, feminists and gender politics. There is a real rhetoric of disorientation in which "gender" has come to be treated as ideology in a historical distortion.[30]

There is a war against everything and everyone, limitless in its goal to serve the capital. This is the working of the neoliberal ideology, itself an unbounded big business, aiming at promoting a lawless society to the benefit of neoliberal "market laws".[31] This service is carried out as a ritualistic promotion of narcotic effect. Fascism is a profound enjoyment

---

[28] Campos, Leonildo Silveira. *Teatro, templo e mercado : organização e marketing de um empreendimento neopentecostal.* São Paulo: editora Vozes, 1997.

[29] www.youtube.com/watch?v=XmDE6jGtfRU

[30] See Tiburi, Marcia. "The Functionality of Gender Ideology in the Brazilian Political and Economics Context." In Conor Foley (ed.) *In Spite of You: Bolsonaro and the New Brazilian Resistance.* New York and London: OR Books, 2018.

[31] Casara, Rubens. *Sociedade sem lei: Pós-democracia, personalidade autoritária, idiotização e barbárie.* Rio de Janeiro: Civilização Brasileira, 2018.

of those who can no longer feel alive because their subjectivities have been destroyed in a historical process of desubjectivation.

Brazil, Neoliberalism and Pandemic

Latin America has long been seen as a "laboratory for the experience of neoliberal policies."[32] Neoliberalism and neo-Nazifascism come together in the project of Jair Bolsonaro, brought to the presidency by militiamen (an increasingly powerful Brazilian mafia), the oligarchies, the bourgeoisie, and the lower middle class. The Brazilian issue becomes even more serious if we remember that there are more than 300 neo-Nazi groups[33] in Brazil that use the swastika as a symbol, and this number is growing. We can already speak of "Nazism" in the Bolsonaro government when we see demonstrations such as that of a secretary of state imitating none other than Joseph Goebbels.[34] The association with ideas and images of so-called "White Power," or US

---

[32] Bandeira, Luiz Alberto Moniz. "As políticas neoliberais e a crise na América do Sul". Revista brasileira de Política Internacional, *Brasília*, Vol. 45, No. 2, pp. 135–46, December, 2002.

[33] The "300 do Brasil," in fact, gathers approximately thirty people led by Sara Geromini, who uses the name of the Nazi socialite Sara Winter (Sara Domville-Taylor, 1870–1944) as her nickname. www.apublica.org/2020/05/especialistas-apontam-semelhancas-entre-os-300-de-sara-winter-e-grupos-fascistas-europeus

[34] The former Secretary of Culture Roberto Alvim, in a video imitating Goebbels, with a similar scenario and costume almost identical to the one used by the Nazi in a speech, quoted the speech of the fascist himself *ipsis litteris*: "Brazilian art in the next decade will be heroic and will be national. It will be endowed with great capacity for emotional involvement and will be equally imperative, since it is deeply linked to the urgent aspirations of our people, or else it will be nothing." In *Goebbels: a Biography* by Peter Longerich (Random House, 2015) we find the following words of the German in the speech quoted by Alvim: "German art of the next decade will be heroic, will be ferociously romantic, will be objective and free of sentimentalism, will be national with great *pathos* and equally imperative and binding, or else it will be nothing."

white supremacism, which derives from the Ku Klux Klan and has representatives all over the world, is growing as well, even though Latin American members are not recognized by Caucasian supremacists as "white." Brazilian "brown" fascists understand themselves as "whites," carrying out racist attacks against blacks. In Brazil, the extreme-right news media has profited a lot from this conjuncture.

If we take into account what Adorno and Horkheimer said in 1947, that technical rationality is the rationality of domination,[35] we understand today's neo-Nazifascism as an enterprise whose success lies in the technological increment allied to capital. We can say that we have moved from an analogical fascism to a digital Nazifascism. The Internet is a market in which people are treated as slaves and commodities at the same time, dominated and made believe as the dominant, maneuvered as agents of hatred and chaos in exchange for emotional compensation. On the social networks each citizen is sold by himself or herself. Someone feeds back in a circuit of spectral recognition, of compensatory "likes" in which narcissism is the stimulant. The ideological explosion of fascism is a marketing and technological explosion that has hatred dissemination in social networks as a proof of its reach, but whose background is the gap of social recognition that the networks offer in an immense narcissistic distortion.

We are facing the functioning of techno-spectral political warfare aiming at psycho-power to promote the annihilation of subjectivity, placing everyone in the position of fascistized robots capable of consuming hatred.

---

[35] Adorno, Theodor; Horkheimer, Max. *Dialektik der Aufklärung. Philosophische Fragmente.* In: Adorno, Theodor Wisengrund. *Gesammelte Werke, Vol. 3.* Frankfurt am Main: Suhrkamp, 1997.

From this point, human action is controlled. Ideology closes all doors to another theoretical and practical imaginary. Thinking reflexively becomes more and more an act of resistance. Linguistic acts are precisely actions whose performativity,[36] that is, the effects they cause in the world, we can understand. Thus, it is the nature of the fascist act that must be analyzed in the context of micro-technology and digital media in order to defeat the current Nazifascism at the moment it establishes itself in our culture.

The digital act is the beginning of our robotization. It is the gesture that defines the new daily form, but it is also the core of a tactic by which the "digital cultural industry" uses the whole of human lives, their thoughts, emotions and actions. The replacement of the schematism of thought by the cultural industry was already a form of psycho-power. In this sense, technical rationality as a form of domination is, itself, the fundamental form of psycho-power.

There will be no overcoming of any kind of fascism if we do not dismantle the strategies of psycho-power, which make use of disinformation and its diffusion in processes of mass desubjectivation, In other words, it is simple "brainwashing,"[37] which today does not need to be carried out with torture procedures, but only with the "torturing" products of the cultural industry and the crazy and narcotic lines of fascist leaders.

In this context, Bolsonaro became a national terror during the 2020 pandemic. While in some countries the incompetence of

---

[36] Austin, J.L.. *How to Do Things with Words* [Como fazer coisas com palavras]. M. Sbisà e J.O. Urmson (eds), Oxford: Oxford University Press, 1975.

[37] Klein, Naomi. *The Shock Doctrine: The Rise of Disaster Capitalism. Picador, 2008.* Klein shows us how brainwashing is produced at the technical level and how it has been used in research in the US and applied to tortures of Latin American dictatorships.

neoliberalism to deal with social issues became evident, in Brazil the bolsonarist neoliberalism acted within the logic of environmental cynicism. It is not an exaggeration to say that the government used the coronavirus to intensify the killing of the population. Bolsonaro's cynical and rude words were available to journalists and anyone on social networks. They became notorious lines stating that the coronavirus was just a "little flu." As the death toll increased and became worrisome, he simply stated: "I am not a gravedigger." Now, infected by COVID-19, many believe that he is only making up a plot in the name of advertising chloroquine,[38] a substance contraindicated by medical researchs and bought in tons by the Brazilian government. The government has stopped counting the death toll and chloroquine, as I write this text, is being sent to the indigenous peoples currently weakened by the COVID-19 and abandoned by the government.[39]

Abandonment and neglect are part of the Bolsonarist government program and no one could think otherwise. For the best specialists in politics, it was simply unimaginable to see someone as like Bolsonaro as president of the Federative Republic of Brazil. Following the rise of fascism in Brazil since 2013 and mindful of the important role Bolsonaro plays in this regard, I will take every opportunity to warn about this unfortunate reality that has prevented me from living in my country since 2018 due to attacks and threats.

Even those who knew that Bolsonaro mimics Donald Trump's strategies under the tutelage of Steve Bannon—who became famous

---

[38] https://www.ictq.com.br/politica-farmaceutica/1554-covid-19-governo-paga-500-a-mais-pelo-insumo-da-cloroquina
[39] https://oglobo.globo.com/sociedade/documento-contradiz-governo-indica-distribuicao-de-cloroquina-em-terras-indigenas-para-combate-covid-19-24519374

for his far-right publicity project active in several countries of the world—could not conceive that his victory was possible. Nonetheless propaganda in the context of the cultural industry of fascism makes everything possible, especially when it devours the sense of politics.[40] Bolsonaro imposed on Brazil the sensation of living in a nightmare, a dystopia increased by the pandemic. There will be no awakening while he remains in office.

If ideology implies a belief without knowledge, in Brazil's case there is an ideology that involves an inability to believe what is common knowledge or to perceive the obvious, because nothing else is hidden in the empire of cynicism. The fate of the country will be the worst as long as it is governed by a project of hatred; and no one can claim that they did not know.

---

[40] Adorno, Theodor. *Die Freudische Theorie und die Struktur der fascistichen Propaganda.* Gesammelte Schriften Vol. 8, T. I [Soziologische Schriften]: Surhkamp Verlag, 1975, pp. 408–33.

1

How to Talk to Fascists—A Title as a Question

When "How to Talk to Fascists" was published in Brazil 2015 many people said I was exaggerating by using the term fascist in the title of my book. My editor at the time did not want to publish it at all. The first edition sold out in a few days, but no one believed that people could be interested in a strange subject such as fascism at that time. I heard people were going to bookstores to hide my book. Which is a curious phenomenon, when it comes to a book on hatred—and against hatred—but which has suffered several attacks of hatred since it was published. Those people were moved by hatred toward the title itself, probably they never read it beyond the cover. People who were unable to understand the irony and provocation of this title were also led to carry out acts based on hatred towards me, in a mixture of misogyny and anti-intellectualism that became a time bomb triggered by the media militias and the extreme-right press and came to explode in 2018 when, persecuted and threatened, I was forced to leave Brazil.

I tell this story here because it is part of the reaction to this book that foresaw and denounced what was to come.

It is a fact that I always had to explain this title, itself an open question. Today, I must say that "How to talk to a Fascist" is an issue that we must seriously consider. At the same time, it is an ironic and provocative phrase. It must be put seriously against its own irony and ironically against its own seriousness. How to talk to fascists is a method and is, at the same time, a question to make us think. This question should not be interpreted as the search for consensus with a fascist, at serious risk of also becoming a fascist, a crypto-fascist, and a potential fascist. The question is, therefore, presented in the sense of provoking us in relation to the extreme of authoritarianism that grows in our society and how we should avoid being part of it.

Although I analyzed the conditions of authoritarianism as a form of human subjectivity, I would like to be wrong about my diagnosis of Brazilian society and the others that relate to the psycho-political phenomenon of fascism that I analyze here.

I called fascism the set of discourses and practices related to hatred, violent communication, and actions that promote the mass killing of people treated as enemies of those who command the opinion of society. Yes, the fascism that this book deals with is a practice that does not work without obedient adherence. In this book, fascism is worked out as content and as a form of action that aims at the annihilation of all difference, the annihilation of the other, and of all that, in the condition of "non-identity," threatens the system that aims to make everything equal and homogeneous. Fascism is an ideology, that is, the lie taken as truth, and it is also "technology," the way the lie is implanted when it must take the place of the truth. In this lies its dependence on propaganda, both in Hitler's time and today, when Fake News and disinformation have returned on a scale that would make Hitler's megalomania jealous.

In writing the first edition of this book, even before the victories of Bolsonaro and Trump, my interest was to understand how fascism was situated at the subjective level of the personality of citizens and how it was able to change the political culture of a nation. The function of the fascistization of democracies, that of serving capitalism and, today, ultra-neoliberalism in its radical phase, needs to be recognized, but my interest was mainly to understand how and by what means the fascist "program" was implanted in people's personalities.

Like many people, I wanted to understand how and why people who gain nothing from fascism, on the contrary, are increasingly unhappy and doomed to failure or extermination precisely by it, paradoxically, adhere to it. The research on the Adorno's Authoritarian Personality[1] had already answered most of my questions, but there was still a lot to think about. I lived in Brazil and saw what was happening to our democracy and I was astonished at the history of Europe before the Second World War seemed to be repeating itself both in the Americas and in other continents and even in my country, which promised to become a better place to live under democratic conditions that had been hard built since the end of the military dictatorship in the 1980s.

My intention with this book, a book of philosophy and not history, is a reflection on the need for those who continue to exist as democratic personalities to move forward, despite the advance of

---

[1] Adorno, Theodor. *The Authoritarian Personality*. Verso Books, 2019.

authoritarian speech. How can we maintain mental health in the face of the familiar and domestic fascism of ordinary citizens and the discourses and practices of those who are their representatives in power? I speak of the drama in which citizens with democratic mindsets meet when they have a relative or friend who fits the F scale (Fascist Scale) that Theodor Adorno talks about[2] that was so important as a source of inspiration for the reflections that I present here. How to survive the fascism that naturalizes itself in everyday life in the world when we know that there is no way to survive fascism when it takes over a country?

"How to talk to a fascist" is not, of course, a practical guide to talking to potential fascists. I do not present here a script for chatting with "authoritarian personalities"—although there are still tips here to keep peace of mind in the face of prejudiced and hateful speech. Depending on the degree of authoritarianism of those involved, a simple conversation may be absolutely unfeasible and a deeper contact in terms of exchanges of ideas may be unthinkable. Even so, this book deals with dialogue, about understanding in order to be able to interact with others and with the world in its current state. Fascism grows in the precariousness of subjectivity until the total destruction of the human world. Dialogue before or after is contrary to fascism and, therefore, it is the antifascist principle par excellence.

---

[2] The F scale or Fascist Scale is a scale for analyzing potential fascism. It is composed of nine elements: conventionalism, authoritarian submission, authoritarian aggression, anti-intellectualism, anti-intraception, superstition and stereotyping, power and "harshness", destructiveness and cynicism, projectivity and exaggerated concerns about sex. Those elements will appear during the book's analysis. See Adorno, Theodor. *The Authoritarian Personality*. Verso Books, 2019.

Performativity and the Fascist Language Game

I tried to present aspects for a reflection on the objective and subjective, linguistic and rhetorical conditions in which fascism develops. One of the fundamental theses of this book is that fascism is a game of language, is the game of language after the "impoverishment" of the experience as a whole due to the impoverishment of language, related to the loss of the ability to tell stories and thus elaborate what was lived, as we can read in the reflections of Walter Benjamin.[3] The richness of language lies in dialogue. Fascism, on the contrary, is the concrete effect of an emotional reality manipulated to obey a rule, a discursive norm that is hate speech. What happens when hatred becomes the rule of a game? As a game, it takes advantage of the lack, of the precariousness of the language that remains to us, which is the very misery of the spirit that, by becoming radical, dresses itself with hate with all the pomp of its arrogance.

To be a fascist is not enough to feel and think like one, it is necessary to practice a "speech act," to speak like a fascist, and it is necessary to act like a fascist. There is, therefore, the performative character[4] of fascism that needs to be better known. Every fascist produces effects

---

[3] Here I am using the concept of "impoverishment of experience" mentioned by Walter Benjamin in his text "The Storyteller". *The Storyteller Essays*. New York Review Books Classics, 2019.

[4] I use the term "Performative" in the same sense as the British philosopher J.L. Austin who defined performative Speech acts that produce concrete effects, which are not just communication, but effective action. See *How to Do Things with Words*, 2nd edn, M. Sbisà and J. O. Urmson (eds), Oxford: Oxford University Press, 1975. See also Judith Butler who uses this concept in *Gender Trouble: Feminism and the Subversion of Identity*, Routledge, 1990.

because that is his way of being. In his study of the Authoritarian Personality—whose book I am quoting—Adorno spoke of a potential fascist, the one who was always in a "state of readiness," that is, ready to leave the sphere of desire or thought and move on to action. Fascists pass to the discursive act, to the action, very easily. Therefore, we can also say that a fascist citizen is in a state of readiness, but also in a "state of propaganda" in relation to his ideology. The act of speech produces symbolic and concrete effects that affect the desire of the other, as must happen with propaganda. A good collaborator of this ideology makes his propaganda without ceasing. There is no relaxation of his duty toward ideology, and even less so in the digital age that absorbs people's time and freedom to think in an unceasing ritual. Thus, any fascist is comfortable and can be exhibitionist at will, because his "state of propaganda" performs very well on current social networks.

Unfortunately, there are people in every family who have their well-hidden hatreds, but who, by perceiving favorable exposure conditions, that is, at the moment when hate speech becomes the dominant trend, are able to manifest themselves, support and even enter into a "fascist trance." What I am calling a fascist trance is something present in street demonstrations in the name of authoritarian leaders that involve the same ecstasy that exists in real lynching and social networks today. No one lives that ecstasy alone. It is the same ecstasy that fueled the hatred in the Nazi concentration camps, the hatred of the torturers in Guantánamo, in the Turkish government's war against the Kurds or in the police in Rio de Janeiro killing black children and youths. The invasion of the US capitol in early 2021 is one example too. It is the ecstasy that arises in destruction and killing that we must also bear in mind in order to understand fascism.

The Act and the Fascist Language Game: Turbofascism

In my opinion, the old fascism has returned. It is the same organized hatred against the other, but under new conditions. A mutation of political culture is on the scene and, although fascism may be eternal as Eco said,[5] it also undergoes historical changes and the great change we live today is digital life. It is clear that we can compare fascism in different countries today, with the fascism of Mussolini and Hitler,[6] but the great difference, in my opinion, is due to the technological conditions of culture. Digital life is made up of what I will call a "digital act," which allows so many people to practice fascist discourse in digital and virtual environments. And it is the nature of the fascist act in the micro-technological and digital conditions of our time that must be analyzed.

The fascist acts of the past were analogical; today they are digital. What does that change in the practice and confrontation of fascism? The capacity to spread propaganda puts us in the face of a turbocharged fascism. It is, of course, a matter of understanding what allows us to move on to such a fascist act, in addition to understanding the nature

---

[5] Eco, Umberto. *Il fascismo eterno. La nave di Teseo*, 2017.

[6] We must not forget that it was Benito Mussolini who gave the name fascism to the movement that developed around him after the First World War and that it were the Italians who used the term "fascio" to denominate the branches or the league between the various branches (the individuals) that had gathered more power. There is nothing too much in this definition, because it reveals only the basic meaning of political power (the idea of union can serve the people, the elites, the minorities), what is curious is how this develops in a conservative and reactionary way and creates a movement around it. See Paxton, Robert Owe. *Anatomy of fascism*. London: Penguin, 2004.

of that act, but we can already state beforehand that the greatest of all the differences that may exist concerns intensity. Now, as a phenomenon, fascism is always produced, it does not arise by spontaneous generation in human subjectivity. It is the conditions of language that allow fascism to arise, therefore understanding the means of language production is so important. The media organizes the order of speech, including fascist speech.

Therefore, it is necessary to understand fascism in the digital age in which social networks define a new space and time. Understanding fascism in the context of the logic of "apparatuses"—to use a concept of Vilém Flusser[7]—that explains that we act within the limits of programming that precedes us. Just as social networks can expand democracy, they can expand authoritarianism. Neither democracy nor authoritarianism are inevitable, they depend on a movement, on what we can define as a "game". It is the concept of play as performativity that we need to keep in mind today.

I speak of game in the broad sense defined by Caillois:[8] staging, toy, set of rules, but also set of things, operation of a gear, structure, dance, movement, way, sport. I also refer to the game understood as in Wittgenstein,[9] as something that is constructed in actions, that is, when meanings of words and sentences arise from the moment they are being used. Today, what we see in the citizens' fascist discourse and in the fascist leaders' speeches on social networks is the manipulation of language game.

---

[7] Flusser, Vilém. *Filosofia da Caixa Preta*. Rio de Janeiro: Reume-Dumará, 2002.
[8] Caillois, Roger. *Les jeux et les hommes. Le Masque et le Vertige*. Gallimard, 1967.
[9] Wittgenstein, Ludwig. *Philosophischen Untersuchungen*. Suhrkamp: 2003

Fascism as a Political Technology—The Unbelievable Brazilian Example Among Many Others

Despite those who dedicated themselves to hating the book and its author, there were also those who, having read the book in 2015, realized its prophetic character. The Bolsonaro danger was already announced far beyond the sad individual figure of the man who came to be president in 2018. The opinion that Bolsonaro was a totally unqualified individual to hold the position he had held as a deputy for almost 30 years without ever having done anything for the people, was a very common one. The vast majority of the population voted for him without knowing who he was. Most likely, people would have voted for anyone who was occupying his role, just as many voted for Trump in the United States.

Those who knew the unwelcoming Brazilian representative were aware he and his sons, all of whom held political positions, were involved in militias and organized crime. His involvement in the murder of Rio de Janeiro's City Councilor Marielle Franco, in 2018, was not a surprise to many people.

However, for the best specialists in political questions, it was simply unimaginable to see someone like Bolsonaro as president of the Republic. Even those who knew about the authoritarianism of Brazilian society, against all the myths of cordiality[10] sold decades ago by theorists who had interpreted Brazil to the liking of the dominant elites, even those people were unable to conceive that the discourse of

---

[10] Holanda. Sérgio Buarque de. *Raízes do Brasil.* Rio de Janeiro: José Olympio, 1971.

hatred could advance so much and that Bolsonaro—and his specialized team—could lead the masses the way he did. Even those who knew that Bolsonaro used the same strategies as Donald Trump, and was guided by Steve Bannon who had worked on his campaign, could not accept that his victory was possible. As I said propaganda makes everything possible. The cultural industry of fascism makes everything homogeneous.[11] The role of propaganda is fundamental in this process.

The use of illegal strategies such as the dissemination of campaign material by WhatsApp with mass shots coming from foreign phone numbers, in addition to a real Fake News production machine against everything and against everyone should not be overlooked. That does not explain much about the election of Bolsonaro, except that it is necessary to define limits and careful vigilance against corruption, including in campaigns that claim to be "anti-corruption," since corruption has become a rhetorical and current "trope". In 2018, Fake News was spread by the digital armies of groups such as the fascists of the MBL (Movimento Brasil Livre[12]), sponsored by entrepreneurs from Brazil and the world. They were scattered by hordes of digital robots, but there was also a lot of

---

[11] Adorno says: "The similarity of the utterances of the various agitators is so great that, in principle, it is enough to analyze the statements of one to know that of all the others". *Die Freudische Theorie und die Struktur der fascistichen Propaganda*. Gesammelte Schriften Vol. 8, T. I [Soziologische Schriften]: Surhkamp Verlag, 1975, pp. 408–33.

[12] The MBL (Free Brazil Movement) emerged in 2014 promoting political actions disguised as moral actions. Sponsored by foreign agents and right-wing parties in Brazil, the movement counted on young hired employees and many volunteers. The head of this movement, Kim Kataguiri, was the protagonist of many actions aimed at gaining notoriety. So they invaded a radio interview in which I participated in early 2018. I refused to remain on the scene and then the next day a wave of Fake News was launched against me lasting for years. In addition to a strong defamation campaign, they broke into every literary event I

spontaneous adhesion from people who were caught like foolish fish on the Internet. The spontaneous adherence and reverberation of fascist ideology is astounding and also needs to be understood.

Given that there is something absurd about these events, the fact that Bolsonaro came to power, and that we are immersed in a nightmare that points to the end of democracy in Brazil as in several countries in the world—is that we must ask ourselves what sustains this current state of affairs.

The extreme right is advancing around the world in places such as the United States, England, Spain, France, Russia, Turkey, Hungary, India, and the Philippines, to name but a few. In these places, populist politicians manipulate the masses in the most diverse ways, but mainly by creating and managing fears. The extreme right is radicalism; it is the ideology and practice of class domination. It grows and manifests itself every time capitalism is under threat. In the same way that racism and sexism advance when classes like blacks and women become more powerful, socially threatening white males, the extreme right cries out every time leftist or social and democratic political perspectives become stronger.

It is evident that it is important to understand "how" Bolsonaro came to power, as well as Trump, and before them, Orban, Erdogan,

---

participated in using various forms of intimidation and even death threats. Now they trying to appear as anti-Bolsonaro, trying to look more right wing than the far right that they really are. Currently social networks such as Twitter have blocked some pages managed by the movement with the aim of spreading Fake News. In 2017, they attempted to close an exhibition called "Queer Museum" produced by Santander Cultural. The curator of this exhibition is currently in exile due to death threats. Several artists were persecuted, among them the Brazilian performer Wagner Schwarz, author of a performance called "La Bête" in which he was nude. The strategy has always been moralistic and psychological in the context of a hybrid war.

Modi, Putin, Duterte, and so many other recent characters who enchant the masses with their nationalist discourses, crude, rude, aggressive, full of violence, xenophobia, racism, misogyny and homophobia, using digital technologies and brainwashing methodologies. Or being just politically incorrect, populist and power hungry like England's Prime Minister Boris Johnson who is also called the English Trump. It is impossible forget Salvini in Italy and the politics of Vox in Spain. It is evident that we must understand the illicit strategies of the uninterrupted campaigns promoted by these characters who are today populist figures, or even tyrannical in power in their countries. These tyrannical-fascist populist politicians govern through social networks as if they were in a constant electoral campaign. Populism means mystification and adulation of the masses, but also the creation of authoritarian masses who blindly follow a leader.

Now, such leaders occupy their time commanding the masses without any action whatsoever to improve their lives. What they do goes through the neoliberal strategies of disaster capitalism[13] with all its attending use of hate speech, including the discourse of shock and imminent catastrophes always caused by people marked as enemies. Such leaders hold on to power through the hypnotic use of a discursive and visual rhetoric that promotes fear and bewilderment while at the same time saying that everything is getting better and better and that they are fighting the "enemy" ("communists," "socialists," "LGBTs" and "feminists").

Specialists from the most diverse areas are analyzing all of this. At the same time, there is an urgent and essential issue at which we need

---

[13] Klein, Naomi. *The Shock Doctrine: The Rise of Disaster Capitalism.* Picador, 2008.

to raise and replace. It concerns understanding the psychosocial and psycho-political conditions of populations that allow these mass manipulators to come to power.[14]

We are talking about something else, by which I mean, the effects of this kind of project. There is, in fact, a project of destruction of the different that is programmed by ultra-neoliberalism. It destroys democracies (only because democracies are different from authoritarianism) throughout the world while democratic groups are unable to resist the wave. Such destruction needs to be analyzed so it can to be stopped. If Brazil is a laboratory of neoliberalism it is certainly the model of something that should be avoided.

In that context, Bolsonaro is a living metaphor. He is a metaphor of authoritarianism that grows by putting Hitler's figure back on the scene. The difference is that Hitler was an overbearing man with artistic and intellectual vanity who wanted to overcome the geniuses of his country. In order to do that he needed to wear certain masks, because the concept of shame was still strong at that time. Bolsonaro is the character of a time when the value of shame has been lost. Just like Trump, Erdogan, Modi, Putin, he is not ashamed of what he says. This lack of shame is strategic in his populism. The ridicule of several of the scenes involving these characters sounds to their followers like heroism. Therefore, this strange heroism of the

---

[14] In this sense, after *How to Talk to Fascists* I published *Political Ridicule* (2017), in which I evaluate the aesthetic strategy of the politics of current fascism and, more recently, a book called *Delirium of Power* (2019) about the specialized production of collective madness that takes over countries by hate speech, the cancellation of rights and the dismantling of institutions that guaranteed democracy. In 2020 I published "How to defeat turbotechnomachonazifascism" (Record).

tyrants of our time has become something "pop" in a process of profound "political mutation."

What is called State Fascism does not exist without a fascism that was previously implanted and took root in the subjectivity of people, and to use perhaps more antiquated terms: in the soul, and in their hearts and minds. The subjective conditions of fascism are always conditions of language, itself the fertile soil of subjectivity. That soil is now being worked in a new way, namely, a technological way. If we consider that the core of fascism is hatred, we need to understand how hatred participates in the processes of language. What happens to hatred under the new conditions in which language once analogical is produced and is today turbocharged by the digital universe? We cannot separate the language from the means by which it is produced, and, in this case, we need to realize that we are seeing new intensities in the production of discourses, precisely because social and cultural conditions have changed as well as the technological conditions.

The absurdity of the situation has provoked a sense of despair in many people. And it is the despairing character that exists at the end of a democracy that we need to face now with our critical reflection. If we do not face fascism, we will continue to be its victims with no chance of defeating it today. Fascists are aware of psycho-power techniques that they use to build their hegemony. Our struggle for democracy needs to be effective against these tactics, but also against this discourse and, at this moment, it is the patience of the reflection that we must invoke. We have to go back to democracy and that means going back to the truth, in other words, taking a step back, to the time before the post-democracy[15] and the post-truth, knowing that a return to the past will only happen as a search for more lucidity in the present.

*

When this book reached the Brazilian gurus of the extreme right wing it was attacked with much verbal violence. Luckily for me, as a writer and teacher, there were many more people who liked it, or were interested in the debate it proposed, than the other way around. That is why the book has been widely read since that year preceding the coup d'état against Dilma Rousseff—and against democracy in my country.

At that time, a publishing house in Germany claimed that it was a "very Brazilian" book and refused to publish it. A book of philosophy also participates in a language game and, in my case, I wrote an intrusive book of denunciation and antifascist positioning. This book can, therefore, only long for the overcoming and failure of its theme, but long for success in overcoming anti-intellectualism—with all hatred for science, art, free thought—which is one of the characteristics of fascism.

Fascism is an unpleasant subject by nature. On the one hand, fascists—in their various degrees of adherence to ideology—do not read books and do not like people talking about fascism; on the other hand, those with democratic mentalities read books, and when they find that one in their hands, they have a strange feeling, a kind of pity to buy a book that they hope, like me, will be overcome as soon as

---

[15] See Casara, Rubens. *Estado Pós-Democrático. Neo-obscurantismo e gestão dos indesejáveis.* Civilização Brasileira, 2017.

possible. In other words, they hope to understand the phenomenon so that they can soon escape it. As an author, I wrote this book in order to collaborate with the effort to overcome the phenomenon and in order to do that, it was necessary to name it, but I hoped that it would be an ephemeral book related to a passing historical phenomenon or that its social political diagnosis, and the prognoses contained therein, would even be wrong. But unfortunately, it has not been like that. Helping to understand fascism, to better act against it, has always been its goal, but I hoped that this goal would be achieved quickly so we could move on to another matter.

The fact that, in my opinion, the reader's affection for the book is also due that I wrote it to vent. The book was the result of a lot of research, of my trajectory as a professor of philosophy and researcher of critical theory, but also of many experiences and a certain ethnology of the culture of daily life that, last few years in Brazil, made evident the advance of the authoritarian personality. This character intensifies day after day and, with the figure of Bolsonaro in power, reaches a catastrophic dimension.[16]

---

[16] Each of Bolsonaro's government ministers defends anti-human rights agendas. The Minister of Education spends his time cursing students and public universities. The Minister of Women and Human Rights spends her time doing religious and sexual mystification attacking gender studies. She said she saw Jesus in a guava tree and that parents in the Netherlands masturbated their baby children as young as a few months old. The Minister of Foreign Affairs argues that he does not listen to military dictatorship and relies on a hatred of communism as do several of those mentioned above. The Environment Minister argues that there are no fires in the Amazon rainforest. Several of them believe the Earth is flat. Jair Bolsonaro has appointed military personnel without any knowledge of the subject to several key ministries. The Ministry of Health is headed by a military person who did not invest even one-third of the amount allocated by Congress to combat the pandemic. Brazil have the largest number of infections and has one of the highest death tolls in the world. There accusations of genocide and crimes against humanity in international courts.

After the coup in 2016, the neoliberal ideology has been implemented at its maximum intensity under the claim of the ideology of the Minimum State, which, as we witness throughout the world, is a Maximum State for the super-rich. It is not impossible for one of these politicians to become the successors of Bolsonaro, because they are all the same. They speak and act in the same way. After all, when we talk about a fascist leader, we are talking about individuals who, in fact, have stereotyped and very simplified mentalities. Unlike those with democratic personalities who are existentially and psychologically complex, the authoritarian personality has something of a pattern that often repeats itself and in whose background there is deep paranoia.

What I say now may seem unimportant; after all, a country like Brazil does not matter much geopolitically. The destiny of Brazil, as well as of all the countries on the periphery of capitalism, from Latin America to Asia, passing through Africa, is to be a colony. In this scenario, I just want to say that, if capitalism is the very and eternal order that always repeats and expands, I will be fighting to break it.

Tropical Fascism—Bolsonaro, Trump, Brazil and the United States

The advance of contemporary fascism is unfortunately no longer new. The "tropical paradise" that Brazil has always been in the world's imagination gave way to an informal authoritarian regime that has been destroying the country. Some speak of "tropical fascism," a questionable expression, given that fascism advances throughout the world, and not only in the "tropics," and is a phenomenon of European origin, related to the ultra-racist idea of a "white supremacy" that influenced Trump's discourse in the United States and that would be absent in the tropical world.

I consider the expression tropical fascism to be worthy of discussion. There is something specific in every appearance of fascism and perhaps even more in the context of the imaginary around a kind of fallacy of the "climatic contrast" in which coldness and rationality are associated with the European character in opposition to the heat that would be proper to the way of being in the tropics. There is nothing more false than that image.

Beyond the fallacies of the geoclimatic imagination, it is a fact that fascism is never the same. It is not equal in the time and space in which it appears. For even if their motivation is the same in historical times, namely, to serve capitalism by butchering the undesirables pre-defined as enemies by the owners of power, there are conditions given in history that define the phenomenon of fascism. We need to better understand those conditions.

In fact, Brazil is not only a "tropical" country from a geographical point of view, infact it is less "tropical" when it comes to human rights that are increasingly disrespected in the current authoritarian scenario. Even today, with the end of fundamental rights such as labor rights and the sale of state-owned companies to foreign entrepreneurs, the Brazilian population will surely become more and more radically impoverished, as has happened in Chile. Brazil is the second most unequal country in Latin America, right after Chile, where the first laboratory of neoliberalism was established in the 1950s with the famous implementation of the economic ideology of the Chicago School. Brazil continues to be this laboratory and its destiny can be traced alongside that of many other countries where economic interests weigh on the territories and its populations.

Similarly, if by tropical we mean "loving" and "warm," "sensual" and "festive," those in power have never been "tropical" with the people. Brazil was always a paradise of the racists. Slavery is a historical fact and a cursed inheritance that has not yet been elaborated and discussed, much less repaired, if indeed it can ever be. Brazil has always been a colony—like all of Latin America—and seems unable to escape that destiny like some other peoples of the world.

What is called "tropical fascism" is a metaphor that emerges in what, in the colonial imagination, is "no-man's-land." As if the native peoples who have lived in Brazil since before the European invasion were not the real owners of that "land." Historically, past and present are erased beneath the image of an imaginary tropical paradise, easily transformed into ideology.

On the other hand, looking at it dialectically, there is something true in the expression, because it refers to something that is part of the imagination about the tropics and that, in fact, is realized as a cultural industry, namely, the idea of relaxing "holidays." The soldiers of neoliberalism, the "internal colonizers"[17] of Brazil, live in scenes of relaxation, on beaches, in swimming pools and at barbecues. Shirtless, drinking beer, as do Bolsonaro and his sons. Bolsonaro appears in

---

[17] Memmi, Albert. *Portrait du colonisé precedé de portrait du colonisateur*. Paris: Gallimard, 1957. The same concept is found in the work of the Bolivian indigenous philosopher Silvia Cusicanqui. See Cusicanqui, Silvia Rivera. *Ch'ixinakax utxiwa : una reflexión sobre prácticas y discursos descolonizadores*. 1st edn. Buenos Aires: Tinta Limón, 2010.

slippers even in the Palace of the Planalto, official residence. It is how he appears on all the social networks. Some love him, others hate him, but for those who know that the power game is nowadays a game of "appearing," it is not difficult to understand the political methodology of populists and their high doses of ridicule.

Trump is the international paradigm to imitate. As "internal colonizer" Bolsonaro follows the external colonizer in a curious sadomasochistic relationship. The sadomasochist pattern is typical of fascist authoritarian personalities. As an example of this sadomasochistic behavior, we see Bolsonaro's strange love for Trump. Now, while I write this book, Bolsonaro has just said "I Love You" to Trump after hours of waiting for a meeting with him. Trump shook his hand. And days later he denied Brazil an invitation to participate in the OECD, thereby humiliating Bolsanaro.

Still, as examples of ridiculous aesthetics of Bolsonaro's political capitalization in his imitation of Trump, which shows the "colonized" pattern of relations between these leaders and their followers, we can cite Bolsonaro's son who, while trying to be Brazil's ambassador to the United States, presented as a credential for the position the fact that he flipped burgers at McDonalds while studying English there. As naive as it may seem to expose oneself in this way and make a fool of oneself, this kind of discourse, in fact has an effect on the masses who feel "seen". The adulation of the masses is a strategy of populists who know how to manipulate a mechanism of identification. And the fascists succeed in the theater of populism because they can praise in the masses what is morally wrong—prejudices, ignorance, violence—without criticism and without any guilt. In the act of talking about frying hamburger as a student, the image of a student on vacation gives way to one who values hard work, humility and wants to prosper. As a theater, it is perfect to provoke a general catharsis in the masses.

In the tropical band of fascism, there is an unrestricted and functional cynicism that consists in speaking atrocities as banalities, in denying any kind of error, in being proud of the errors, in never assuming guilt. The minister of justice in Bolsonaro's government is one of the best examples. Confronted with the crimes he commits himself, he simply states, "There's no problem at all." Evidently cynicism represents the most advanced moment of laughter with which everything begins. All the fascist tyrants in power today can make it appear that cynicism is a sign of authenticity.

In the tropical side of fascism, the production of laughter is encouraged. Philosophers from Aristotle to Bergson mentioned the cathartic effect of laughter, with its potential for sublimation in relation to pain and suffering. At the same time, it was because of laughter that the people elected Bolsonaro and Trump. At first they seemed like clowns. It is as if, these days, catharsis has changed its meaning. Today, catharsis no longer means releasing the cry that frees one from suffering, but releasing the cry that destroys suffering while also destroying the object. It is hate that wants to be liberated to exist, and not love, because as love no longer exists, it is no longer produced. Behind it is the story of resentment, of everything that was not elaborated, of an education for coldness.[18]

---

[18] Adorno, Theodor. "Education After Auschwitz," *Critical Models: Interventions and Catchwords*, trans. Henry W. Pickford. New York: Columbia University Press, 2005.

In fact, no matter how many reasons, we find to criticize the expression "tropical fascism," it is not so absurd. If we read it with dialectical attention, there is something about what has been happening in Brazil that reminds us of *Apocalypse Now*. Although the film takes place in Vietnam, it presents the "hot" landscape that is present in this ideological imagined tropic. The scene of the bombing of a peasant village to the sound of Wagner's "Ride of the Valkyries" is a direct reference of Nazism in Coppola's film. The governor of Rio de Janeiro promoted helicopter shootings over slums killing several people. This became common in 2019. We don't know if the police hear any music while they kill people in the favelas of Rio de Janeiro, including children, but the similarity is terrifying. Meanwhile, racist killings of young blacks continue in the United States and in all countries where the "enemy" is defined by "color" and "race." In Brazil, where there should be no xenophobia—after all, Brazil is a country built by immigrants rejected from Europe and the diaspora of enslaved African peoples—there have been expressions of xenophobia against Haitian and Venezuelan immigrants.

Resentment and Mimicking

The fascist individual is unable to relate to his own history of pain. Cold is a sufficient affection in his experience. The impossibility of elaborating his own history of accumulated suffering, including the education that allowed him to become an authoritarian subject, is what sustains his resentment. Resentment is the type of feeling that returns, precisely because it has not been elaborated. Because we do not elaborate our feelings and emotions, we can become potential authoritarian and fascist personalities. And why don't we do that? We do that, because our culture is a culture of coldness. Capitalism derives from this culture and repeats it.

Class resentment—the horror of poverty and the poor—was a fundamental factor in the advance of Nazism in Germany and is still at work in our time. In all the countries where it returns today, fascism implies a hatred of the poor by the middle class up to total contempt for the same classes on the part of the economic elites. The poor are often led to hate themselves, as in the case of soldiers and policemen who are the agents of slaughter in the various countries where state violence is at work. They are poor people who kill the poor at the behest of the State.

Not looking poor, indeed looking as something unresolved aesthetically like someone from rich classes, erasing the social and historical fact of poverty, is a gesture from which fascism takes advantage. Thus, we can understand how a poor person is capable of defending capitalism without realizing that it is its executioner. It is better to identify with him in order to erase the very pain of being his victim. The imitation of the rich becomes a strategy.

The middle class of fascist countries imitates the rich of the world in prefabricated fantasies. The "American Way of Life" is the style to be emulated, because only it guarantees the integration to capitalism— capitalism as style, or the "Capitalist Realism" as we see in the art of Sigmar Polke.[19] The one who is integrated feels protected. This

---

[19] The movement Capitalist Realism was created in the 1960s in Berlin as a reaction to American Pop Art. Artists also associated with "capitalist realism" are Gerhard Richter, Manfred Kuttner and Konrad Lueg.

aesthetic phenomenon is related to conscious and unconscious aspects. The fact that all fascists and tyrants look like Trump, even if it is only in speech, is not a pure chance in the aesthetic barbarity we have seen for so long. Everything becomes the same in fascism, because it is a product of the cultured industry of politics.

There is a social mimicry that makes it possible to compensate for the terrible feeling of being one who is in poverty or in unfavorable geopolitical conditions. This sensation is the resentment expressed by the emotion of hatred. Fear walks beside everyone, the fear of becoming poor that characterizes the emerging middle class, or, as Adorno tells us, the attachment to privilege that is the result of a subjective class consciousness.[20] For this reason, the middle class needs such a criterion as the distinction it achieves through the aesthetic path of illusions. They imitate the ways of life, but they also imitate the dominant classes' words, including their prejudices.

The aesthetic imitation of the rich that leads people to wear branded clothes like the rich wear, ride in luxury cars like the rich do, eat in fashionable restaurants and travel according to the lifestyle of the rich, to look like they have purchasing power and thus "achieve" social capitalist respectability, quickly turns into imitation of their speech. Those who cannot buy as their models or esterotypes, they can at least speak imitating their ideas. The cultural industry updates all this for the poor. It makes accessible any merchandise that can contemplate this systematic imitation. In this context, it is the

---

[20] Adorno, Theodor. *Aspekte des neuen Rechts-Radikalismus.* Surhkamp, 2019.

discourse of hatred that, on social networks, works for many as a kind of school uniform.

The dream of "Traveling to Miami" is part of the task to imitate rich Americans in their beach houses with designer cars in the garages. The "dream of consumption" of many Brazilians is a compensatory fantasy. In the impossibility of realizing this dream, there are substitutes for money within the reach of the less-wealthy hands. There is a whole aesthetic to be respected—a whole set of rules to emulate looking like an American—which would mean being "bourgeois" and not poor, being white and not black, being heterosexual and not homosexual. And to complete this aesthetic standard, an ethical and moral standard is constituted at the discursive level. In the fascist middle class houses, the killing of the poor, blacks, indigenous people, popular leaders, women and LGBTQI+—either by hunger or by weapons—is lived as a party in environments marked by bad taste decoration.

Among those groups where mimicry is the rule, many people who voted for Bolsonaro did so only because Trump was elected in the United States. The power of influence of American popular culture over Brazil is immense and we can say that [is also the case?] across the world. The mimicry represents compensation, it is a kind of defense mechanism in the context of a shattered self-esteem that Brazilians have in relation to themselves. The feeling of abandonment and rejection is one of the most important factors in the formation of resentment and in Brazil it is expressed at the national level in a colonization never assumed and always disguised.

The "Wall" as a Xenophobic Ritual in the Age of the Spectacle

Politics has always been somewhat of a theater in which its characters have always been fundamental. Kings, emperors and popes have always had their spectacular rituals to produce certain effects. All power has its aesthetics. Hitler would not have advanced in Germany if he were not an expert in mass mystification like all fascist leaders, and this does not happen without the pomp of rituals of mass enchantment. At the time of what Guy Debord called the "society of the spectacle,"[21] when image is the capital and is also valid for its value of circulation, the mystification is a breakthrough. Today, mystification is much easier than it was before the invention of television and the Internet with its power of diffusion.

Trump, Bolsonaro, Duterte, Modi, Johnson and others are specialists in causing effects. They occupy daily news with absurd speeches. Their central rhetoric is the fallacy of reduction to absurdity. The reason is something eliminating. They say absurd things to touch people's sensibilities. Everything is continually treated as if the principles of these governments were the political campaign. It is a policy of mental and corporal shock. The campaign cannot be interrupted to give way to other relevant ideas and discussions. Politics is reduced to propaganda. It is necessary to keep citizens' minds occupied and the life practices that revolve around the "great leader." Thus, Trump and his pathetic companions make speeches

---

[21] Debord, Guy. *La Societé du Spectacle*. Gallimard, 1996.

aimed at drawing attention to themselves, always trusting in the citizens' lack of discernment.

Xenophobia against Mexicans was one of the fundamental axes of Trump's campaign and government, as well as terrorism and other anti-Western slogans, because it is an issue that generates a direct controversy and a direct emotion in its voters. Hate is that direct emotion.

The wall on the border with Mexico is a way to understand what fascist mystification is all about in the age of spectacularization. The wall has a complex function. It updates the American fascist myth par excellence, which is the very white supremacy in the United States formalized in Jim Crow's segregationist laws. From the fascist perspective, it is not enough to create an unjust or perverse law to be fulfilled if this law does not collaborate with the process of spectacularization necessary for power to remain in place. It is evident that it should not be said that all power is fascist, but that a perverse level of authoritarianism marks it. Fascism, in turn, implies the entrance onto the scene of madness—of an insane character—in the games of power.

Trump's speech on the wall with Mexico is exemplary. It just sounds like authoritarianism, but at the same time the delusional nature of his stance is at play. While rational people are concerned about safe immigration and some are proposing to open borders completely due to economic and ecological issues, Trump insists on building an uneconomical and anti-ecological wall. Many people follow, but ignore the damaging effects of construction. In fact, it seems unreasonable to close absolutely a gigantic border between two countries in the middle of the twenty-first century. We always hope that good arguments overcome brute force and stupidity in a democratic scenario. Today's tyrants exploit the paradox of democracy through which they elect themselves and yet which they abhor.

If fascism has to do with "myth," with the appropriation of data, facts or images, and even with ancient narratives, it also has to do with tragedy. Tragedy, in turn, is something related to ritual, which in itself already implies staging. Tragedy is the staging of sacrifice. Thus, the enemy must be sacrificed in a ritual visible to all. Now, Trump's wall may even have the practical, authoritarian and xenophobic purpose of avoiding the presence of many immigrants, but its main function is symbolic, it is the ritual function. In the case of the wall, Mexicans are "sacrificed" because they could not go to the USA to survive. The image of a Mexico from which people want to escape and of a USA where it is desirable to live is exploited by this separation. The opposition of "us" and "them" is like the opposition of "Hell vs Paradise," and like all known binarism and dualisms.

The ritual function has an aesthetic character. It operates in the capture of attention, sensitivity and consciousness. Trump rescues outdated ideas to ensure the ritual. The old ideology of "America First," an American nationalist movement of the 1940s—highly pro-fascist and anti-immigration—was brought back with all its segregationist charge. Trump also rescued the slogan "Make America Great Again" created in Ronald Reagan's first campaign in 1980, to delight the masses moved by slogans. As this is a very old-fashioned idea, which affects a lot of people, nationalism has a mystifying validity and therefore it gives way to xenophobia which is much more pragmatic, because it involves the racist element and the fear of job losses, considering that this is one of the concrete fears of the middle class, although there is no sense in it. Nationalism, in turn, also comes into play, also as an old idea that returns to the surface.[22] This is something meaningless in the era of globalization, when people are interested in traveling, in crossing borders, in learning more languages than ever before. Also this fear of the "other" as a foreigner can be mystified by the economically and culturally humiliated classes. The economic elites take advantage of this.

Whatever the example, we can see that politics has been reduced to propaganda. Publicity today has the role of mystification; it is the path of sacrifice. Its success lies precisely in the promise of a return to a heroic and paradisiacal past as opposed to an infernal present in which Mexicans are demonized. "Demonizing" is a rhetorical practice, that is to say, it is a performative practice that aims to produce spectacular effects, which is part of the history of authoritarianism and fascism. What Hitler did was demonize the Jews, just as the Catholic Church demonized women as witches in the sixteenth and seventeenth centuries, as Silvia Federici showed us.[23] By the way, the alliance between fascism and sexism is evident, both because women must serve the reproduction of the species, as in Nazi ideology, and because, by refusing to participate, they must be exterminated. What we see in Margaret Atwood's famous book *The Handmaid's Tale*[24] is a great representation of what fascism can do to women. Today, authoritarian institutions demonize "gender" in the same way that it is necessary to destroy analytical categories and fields of study that expand the democratic space.

---

[22] Stanley Jason in his book *How Fascism Works: The Politics of US and Them* (Random House, 2018) develops an interesting analysis of the topic of nationalism.

[23] Federici, Silvia. *Caliban walks the Witch*. New York: Autonomedia, 2004.

[24] Atwood, Margaret. *The Handmaid's Tale*. Boston: Houghton Mifflin Harcourt, 1986.

The fascist formula is always the same, to resurrect something from the past to stimulate a mythical feeling in the citizens. To recover the tragic staging of the life. Now as an illusion, that is to say, the same reason that made Hitler invent a relationship with the Aryans and make the swastika the symbol of his movement by placing himself, moreover, as the center of that movement.

Whatever the prejudice, the hatred exposed in the speeches of these leaders and their followers, whether sincere or not, has the function of mystifying, of moving people toward their most primitive affections and thus imprisoning them. There is a mental colonization that counts on the fertile soil already prepared by the cultural industry which aims at the standardization of thought, perception, feelings and behavior. In this sense, contemporary fascism is identical to the fascism of Hitler and Mussolini who provided their followers with ready-made ideologies.

All these leaders, who take their place as tyrants elected by the people, have their advisors and co-religionists, their Goebbels and Himmlers, their Torquemadas. No fascism survives without heavy propaganda. For this reason, because it is not a natural phenomenon that spontaneously sprouts in societies, as the purchase of a bottle of Coke or a snack from McDonalds is not, we need to understand where it comes from, what it serves and under which conditions it is sustained in order to avoid social, ethical and political tragedies from continuing to repeat themselves.

Ridiculous as the Core of Fascist Propaganda

The feeling of perplexity that arises in us when we see the actions of certain characters in various positions of political power could be defined as "Political Ridiculous." It is a kind of "universal shame" on the part of citizens who feel responsible and concerned about democracy. Meanwhile, those who occupy the positions of representation feel no shame at all. It is as if democracy has been reduced to a communal sharing of the shame we have on behalf of our representatives. These characters exist in many countries and in most of them they become presidents, prime ministers, deputies or assume positions of power in the media. Politicians constantly come from mass media or churches that serve as a space for the most important part of their entire political project, the propaganda.

One question that arises for everyone is: how can these politicians become presidents? The cult personality of the fascist leader praises characteristics such as simplicity, sincerity and spontaneity. My hypothesis is that it does not matter if they are spontaneous or not, the fact is that the theater they play, the scene they build, serves as a factor of political capitalization. Therefore, what brings these politicians to power is not something like the simple and natural fascism of the masses, but their strategy of mystification that includes a fascination for their way of being, and this is insurmountable when it comes into play in politics. It is impossible to deconstruct the cult of fascist personality because it is about a transference relationship in which the leader is taken as the father who is far beyond a figure who loves and hates. That "father" is a figure who is obeyed in a sadomasochistic way.

Jair Bolsonaro spent his life making outlandish statements and, at the same time, becoming popular because of them. He became such a stereotypical character that people laughed at him. He was a laughing stock, like Trump. But while people were making jokes, they took advantage of it to become popular. At the same time, those who criticized them fell into the trap of making them even better known. This shows that propaganda is a kind of inescapable founding principle of fascism. We can say that not all propaganda is fascist, but that no fascism resists without propaganda. The question that remains is: how can people have cognitive and conceptual access to how propaganda acts on them?

Bolsonaro says a lot of bizarre things. Once he said, for instance, "A policeman who doesn't kill, is not a policeman." And another time, he said, "I would be incapable of loving a homosexual son" and too "I prefer to see my son dead". The things he says are very serious, but as he says it in a way that does not convince many people, it seems that he is always being ironic. Many, however, agree with him. He charmed the masses and went on to be used by the media and by the clever people of the neoliberal economy because he always behaved as if he were a fool. That is the difference between Trump and Bolsonaro and other tyrants as Erdogan from Turkey, Orban from Hungary or Modi from India. Bolsonaro and Trump succeed much more because they look "weak" than because they look "strong." And, in that case, the question is the cultural circumstances and conditions to develop the basic elements of fascism. He continues to resort to ridiculousness to rule, surrounding himself with characters who behave in an equally ridiculous manner, including ministers who believe that the earth is flat and one minister who once said she met Jesus in a guava tree.

In Bolsonaro's case, ridicule is a natural pattern. He is much more in his way of speaking, his pimping expressions, his stupidity expressed in his speech. If on the one hand, he says that people who want to protect nature should "poop every other day," on the other hand, he goes to a ceremony in Japan, dressed in an absolutely inappropriate way. This way, it bothers some people, but it pleases those who identify with it. What he does is to confuse all the people who do not understand his populist strategy. I don't mean by this that he plans all his actions aesthetically, but that certainly these characteristics, instead of knocking him down, have made him advance. The fascist rise needs this kind of character fit to be the main factor of mystification and the core of the propaganda. Bolsonaro also serves as an "advertising man" of the arms industry: his first act as a president was to release weapons in Brazil. His advertising gesture, the hallmark of his campaign, is to make the sign of a weapon with his hand. All the politicians who imitate him in Brazil easily elect themselves as it happens everywhere in the world, as those who made the Nazi greeting were capitalized in Hitler's time.

Bolsonaro and Trump spend their time practicing a kind of psychological terrorism, seeking daily to shock and impress everyone. Social networks are very important to these new populists because they are accessible and have entered the lives of all social and cultural classes. In this way, we can say that it is as if they govern minds through "virtual" decrees, while behind their spectacles, the real neoliberal government develops with specialists in dismantling the welfare state and destroying acquired rights and public policies. People increasingly reject Bolsonaro's repugnant policies, but the mystification, as to how he gained his power, continues today.

In a global context, Brazil is a laboratory for the extreme right, testing ways to reach the whole of political culture and to leverage economic power. This project knows the fragility of democracies and does not tire of abusing it. Therefore, we must carefully analyze what has been happening in such countries in that authoritarianism rises from ways that seems democratic. We know that these exaggerated performances are characteristic of exhibitionist tyrants and that all authoritarianism requires some level of theatricality. But we also know that in democratic regimes, in which people should have the best chance to advocate for themselves, masses of voters choose the worst and most pathetic politicians. Because this theatrical production of ridiculousness is the means by which voters are manipulated into cynicism, there is need for greater analysis.

In 2017, I used this idea of the "Political Ridiculous" as the framing for my book *Political Ridiculous* in which I warned of the danger of Bolsonaro when no one could believe that he would evolve from an insignificant parliamentarian into the nation's president. I understand by "political ridiculousness" a mutation in the current political culture. This mutation is complex, but it occurs especially in the aesthetic field of political existence. In other words, it means that the theatrical dimension—of images, of the spectacular, of public rallies—counts now more than ever. Such theatrics suffer from a distortion linked to the concomitant infantilization of society. Ignorance and ridiculousness generate a strange empathy and become significant political capital.

Politics always implies a scenario, a backdrop; it implies the way in which costumes, speech and gestures of the political actors develop within scenes. But there is an even deeper aspect. The cultural industry of politics specializes in managing sensations and controlling mentalities and sensibilities. And now this industry has begun to bet on the empathy generated by the Political Ridiculous.

The Political Ridiculous is the scene in which pathetic and ignorant actors take the lead and exercise power when many do not take politics seriously. These politicians say they are not politicians, and many citizens fall into the trap of voting and supporting them without realizing the self-contradiction within these characters who say they do not do what they do. People cannot understand why they are victims of a cynical strategy.

If we want to understand politics today, we need to understand how these characters have built their position as protagonists. While Trump built an image of success in business, Bolsonaro was practically unknown to most Brazilians. For nearly 30 years he was an unproductive congressman without any importance in the political scene. But he knew how to be cynical—and how to capitalize on the ridiculous. Suddenly, he began to appear in the public consciousness. He grabbed headlines after he made homophobic attacks against a gay congressman (who today lives in exile in Europe). Later, his misogynistic attacks directed at a congresswoman—saying, "I wouldn't rape her because she was very ugly"—somehow made him more famous[25]. Condemned by some, followed by others, he gained space and presence in the press, and that was all he needed to go further.

Politicians elected from the anti-political discourse, made politics while denying it at the same time. It is a rhetorical game that needs cynical performativity. They won in a strange zone, that of contradiction, and self-contradiction, in which the game of the cynical circle positions some in the place of the cynical exploiters, while others are the exploited. In the first case, the contradiction is used in their favor, in the second, one falls into it believing that one has some advantage with it. It is the

---

[25] Guardian, 'Brazilian congressman ordered to pay compensation over rape remark', Guardian, 18 September 2015 https://www.theguardian.com/world/2015/sep/18/brazilian-congressman-rape-remark-compensation.

old dialectics of the master and the slave[26] (or lordship and bondage), which has taken on a new form: it has been replaced by a kind of cynical, negative and unsolved dialectics. In that version, power and freedom are at stake in the struggle between the parties, the dispute between those who rule and those who obey was the struggle of desire that would emancipate the strongest, the desire itself.

The discourse of anti-politics is present in these contexts. Anti-politics is the reduction of politics to propaganda against politics itself. The game is one of cunning and cleverness. Propaganda hides the contradiction and politics takes advantage of it. Depoliticization is a partial name to speak of the empty advertising of political action produced and intensified by discourses and institutions. This is, at the same time, the new politics, the politics depoliticized by advertising that is presented as the true and best politics that could ever have existed.

The lack of interest in politics on the part of the vast majority of people, the huge number of people who refuse to vote, many times greater than the number of first runners in the race, is a clear sign of what is happening in a political culture profoundly altered by advertising. Politics is a commodity doomed to failure.

The rejection of politics is not spontaneous. It came about with the collaboration of discourses and practices of all institutions. But what is the point of eliminating politics? Or who is served by the abandonment of politics? There are individuals and groups who

---

[26] Hegel, G.W.L. The theme of "Master-slave dialectic" is a formulation present in the Phenomenology of Hegel's Spirit to explain the emergence of self-awareness and desire. The text deals with the struggle for recognition as a life and death struggle between two subjects. Dialectics resides in the recognition that one does not exist without the other.

contribute with speeches and practices to the deterioration of the sense of politics, but who do not distance themselves from it. They remain in politics: they stand as candidates, they are elected, and they fight for power. They play the political game on the cynical side. The people have their place as fools.

Then there is the curious case of those who were elected, those who depended on the vote of the people, but do not represent the people at all. The sense of democracy as a government of people is, of course, set aside by many people, who have been led to believe that "without politicians and politics" is better. When they say that without politics it is better, they do not stop making politics; they only do "the politics of no-politics." A policy misrepresents its meaning, and misrepresents democracy itself. They fall into contradiction, but nothing happens to them. Because, in the context of the cynical circle that is the way things work.

Cynicism is the act and the effect of the contradiction carried out and used in favor of the one who committed it. Cynicism is an attitude, that of who is completely true, according to ancient scholars who practiced "parrhesia,"[27] the act of speaking what one thinks, no matter who it hurts. However, the truth is also a value and, as such, it changes historically. In the post-truth era, we can say that a cynic is a subject who always manifests as completely "post-truth."

We live in a time when truth is no longer a virtue. Cynicism, therefore, has also changed. Today, it puts itself in the place of the true posture, since the truth no longer has any value, which is why so many are speaking now in post-truth. It is about the true with no value of

---

[27] Foucault, Michel. *Le Courage de la vérité. Le gouvernement de soi et des autres.* Seuil, 1984.

truth or, if not, true as value of true. Therefore, when we see someone quietly speaking a lie as if it were true and as if there were nothing wrong with it, it is not just a simple self-contradiction. That is why it is so easy to become confused and inert when faced with a cynic. One cynical person is telling the truth and lying at the same time, and at the same time he or she is not telling the truth and he or she is not lying. What is someone doing then? He or she is deceiving, but not only that. He is turning the other into a sucker, positioning someone in a place where he or she can only stand linguistically still inert. The cynic creates the web in which the sucker will be devoured.

The clever emerge and use cynicism as a deceptive tactic. It is the most effective of all tactics when it comes to power in times of the defilement of democracy. An act of language, both verbal and performative, cynicism is a posture and the cynic occupies a special place within it. Every single one of the authoritarian leaders of our time use this tactic, as did the authoritarian leaders of the past. All, invariably, place themselves in the posture of an unquestionable sovereign with the objective of demonstrating moral, emotional and brutality strength. Therefore, the cynical tyrants of our "pseudo-democracies" do not renounce it. It is true that they use violence all the time against their enemies, but this happens under a cynical smokescreen. Their cynical stance is absolutely resistant to criticism. Criticism comes, but it has no effect on the cynic.

Now we have the dialectic between the cynic and the sucker. That is an inevitable relationship after politics suffered an intense emptiness. It is the quality of the political relationship that has changed. Now the master is the cynic and the slave is the sucker. There is no longer a struggle for power or freedom because the sucker is the slave who has no chance of winning. Having a chance would be like having a conscience, but it has been annihilated. Poisoned by endless of television programs, doped by neoliberal religious, by offers in the field of consumption, the sucker—adulated as a consumer—is not capable of turning the game around because he is not aware of what they do with it. Consciousness is what frees the cynic, and yet it is unavailable. It would be a kind of antidote, but without irony it is literally missing from the market.

The fact is, anybody gets no reaction in front of a cynic. He ends up with his opponent, putting him in the position of an idiot. And to put him there, he just puts on the cynic's mask.

How does the cynic achieve this feat of putting everyone else in the position of suckers? Helping to form suckers, preparing the ground on which dialectics will transform the sucker into a new cynic. A cynical community is approaching. All authoritarianism is fertile soil and, by fertilizing it with cultural industry and market religion, we know that the expected result will reach success.

Who are the suckers of our time? There are suckers in all spheres, in all professions and institutions. The sucker is formed by a cynical and manipulative media and religion, he is prepared to believe in everything they offer within a program of rejection of what is different (generically understood as something aesthetic, ethical, cognitive and political). He never asks himself, because doubt, not being useful, is not offered by the cynical system.

Cynics set the trap of the non-political, suckers are the those who fall for the praise of life without politics. The suckers satisfy the cynics. Dialectically speaking, they may even become cynical at some point. The power they gain in an opportunistic way. The discourse that politics is over, that politicians are all corrupt, is the discourse that the sucker gets as a gift from the cynic, created by the great system of production of cynicism that is capitalism in its political action. It is as if the cynic has warned that power has an owner and that this owner is not the people to whom he speaks.

Everyone who fall into spontaneous ideologies sustain the cynical circle of power: the poor who defend neoliberal values, homosexuals who defend homophobic politicians, and women who defend misogynists. They are not a novelty of our time, or of a single country. There are peoples—and masses— that like that everywhere.

The cynic does not need to deceive in order to deceive. Cynical performance is that of one who hides something that, at the same time, he shows. Democracy is now reduced to an aesthetic procedure (advertising dressed up as politics, like the wolf in sheep's clothing). Democracy ceases to be narrated from the point of view of tragedy and comedy and becomes a bad joke.

2

Potential Fascism

What I call a "potential fascist" from a definition by Theodor Adorno is a very common psycho-political type of our time. Its characteristic is to be politically poor precisely because it is affective, reflective and linguistically poor. This impoverishment of the spirit is not a fault of someone. Nobody is born that way. Every citizen who adheres to fascism has been forged in a social context. Which is not only historically concrete, but psycho-politically complex. Adorno spoke of a fascist as being in a state of readiness, always able to leave the sphere of pure fantasy and move on to the act. I will use the same definition when talking about this subject without political autonomy and yet free, with whom we live again at that moment in all corners of the world.

The impoverishment of the experience as the impoverishment of the language of which it is the bearer was due to the loss of the dimension of dialogue, a loss in terms of living with the difference. Dialogue becomes impossible when the dimension of the other is lost. The figure of the fascist cannot relate to other dimensions that go beyond the absolute truths on which one has established his way of being. The lack of openness, proper to the fascist personality easy to recognize in everyday life, corresponds to a fixed point of view which serves against people and facts that do not correspond to pre-established worldview of that kind of personality.

It lacks the dimension of otherness. The other is reduced to a function within the circle in which fascist subjectivity entangles it. Perhaps like the spider which sees in the fly only the food that serves it and which therefore needs to be captured in a web.

The other, denied, sustains the fascist in his certainties. The function of certainty is to deny the other. And to deny the other comes to be a totally unethical practice which leads to the production of truths aimed at denying the alterity. There is a vicious circle. To disentangle oneself from it may be impossible, because in our time the lack of interest in the truth[1] has reached an abnormal dimension. And the lack of interest in ethics—which would be its correspondent dimension—seems to accompany all this.

When I talk about otherness, it is about opening up to the other. Closed in on itself, a fascist personality cannot perceive the "commonality" that exists between itself and the other, between "me and you." The fascist personality does not mentally and emotionally form the notion of something that can be understood as "common," which is shared between different beings. For this notion to be established, we depend on something that happens with an opening to the other, but from which can be barred by the fear of the other. The "common" is complex, it is as much what we "use" in one game with the other, as what someone want for a game to happen. Fascist would be the trace of that person in emotional, verbal and concrete

---

[1] Frankfurt, Harry. *On Truth*. Alfred A. Knopf, 2006

warfare against social ties while sustaining authoritarian relations, relations of domination that impede the right of the other to presence and even existence. All this can be summed up in ethnocentrism, which is a basic form of "racism" and, in my view, of paranoia and, therefore, of delirium, and sometimes it turns into nationalism, even if it is only a surrenderist and colonial nationalism like that of Bolsonaro.

The research on Theodor Adorno's Authoritarian Personality gives us insight into common aspectos of what Adorno and his fellow researchers have called the "authoritative syndrome." The so-called F Scale or Fascist Scale is a list of parameters for understanding authoritarianism in different combinations and intensities in the type of personality that tends to be undemocratic. In Adorno's view, all these traits are somehow linked to ethnocentrism with all that it entails in terms of a kind of paranoid excuse, that is, an inability to escape the delirium at the center of which is the "I" as a weight and, of course, not as a poetic fact. The traits are as follows: (1) conventionalism (rigid adherence and obedience to the traditional values of the middle class, moralism); (2) authoritarian submission (to the idealized moral authorities of the group itself); (3) authoritarian aggression (the tendency to be alert, condemn and punish people who do not share conventional values); (4) anti-intraception (opposition to a subjective and sensitive mentality and to all that it represents, such as a love for the arts, knowledge and science, anti-intellectualism); (5) power and harshness (affirmation of strength and harshness, concern with the domain–submission dimension); (6) superstition and stereotyping (rigid and unquestionable values, belief in destiny); (7) destructiveness and cynicism (vilification, radical evil, desire for death and annihilation of the other, Fake News and slander); (8) projection (expression of unconscious impulses); and (9) excessive concerns about sex. Adorno comments on all of these traits and how they were arrived at in research carried out with groups of Americans in the 1930s and 1940s and published in 1950. These are traces that appear even today. We can consider that these traits are still present in the form of current fascism. My goal is not to analyze each one of them, but to express them so that we can use them—without rigidity—as categories of analysis within the scope of our reflection.

What remains present in all these examples is hatred and rejection of the "other." The other must be destroyed, which the authoritarian personality would do, if it were possible, by means of a magical act, that of speech. One of the pleasures of hatred is its exposition; hate speeches produce pleasure, but they are also carried out as magical acts, which power realization. In fact, the exhibition is the catharsis of hatred that generates more hatred. The "exposure value" of which Walter Benjamin spoke[2] finds another function in our time, that of emotional compensation, which is, at the same time, political. The authoritarian or fascist subjectivity uses the destructive affection of hatred to cut potential ties, while sustaining, through hatred, the submission of the other in a truly sadomasochist scheme. We therefore have the impression that fascists are all crazy, because they live in trance and ecstasy, exposing themselves through speeches that embarrass many people, offend people with democratic personalities and produce victims of prejudices and crimes such as racism and homophobia.

---

[2] Benjamin, Walter. *Work of Art in the Age of Its Technological Reproducibility, and Other Writings on Media.* Harvard University Press, 2008.

In our time, we have learned to separate the moral sphere from that of madness. The goal was to protect people who suffer from mental ilness. In Freud, and also in Lacan, there would be no reason to make someone who suffers from mental illness, a subject free of responsibility. So, I would like to bring up one more question for us to think about fascism. In fact, we cannot say that fascists are crazy. Or rather, that they are just crazy. But madness can be a valid category of analysis through which to understand politics.

Adorno's recently published commentary in a text from the late 1960s about the extreme right, about a "residue of incorrigibles or madmen, a lunatic fringe"[3] which cannot be separated from the authoritarian system, seems to make perfect sense in the current climate. What kind of psycho-political subject would be unable to support democratic regimes? We can talk again about the "eternal return" of the same, of a repressed that comes to the fore, both in historical and psychoanalytic terms to understand the question, but the most philosophical idea that the fascist movements are a wound, a scar in democracy that has never been up to its own concept, seems to me the clue that we must follow. That is precisely why fascism can return, because democracy has not been consolidated. Because there are disruptive personalities who have never been able to connect with democracy. However what to do? How can we educate a person to democracy? The return of fascism is proof of the failures related to democracy. In reflecting on this, we may discover that democracy is a dynamic process, that it needs to be reconstructed every day, that it

---

[3] Adorno, Theodor. *Aspekte des neuen Rechts-Radikalismus.* Berlin: Suhrkamp, 2019.

depends on individual, collective, legal and state gestures, and that only in this way will we achieve the politics we desire as the democratic beings that we wish to be.

The function of the ever-exposed speeches and wicked acts is certainly to safeguard the cold emotion of the leader, without which the leader would collapse. The fascist theater, or the performative environment around it, implies exposure, ritual, trance, and ecstasy. It is as if everyone should enter into madness, participate in the demential articulation, in the system of madness (Wahnsysteme[4]) around the leader. The masses need a focus for their sadomasochistic actions: each one must be submissive to the leader and be aggressive with the "enemy." By reproducing this logic, the leaders who command the masses are guaranteed success. Looking from the outside, everyone seems crazy in a generic sense of the term madness. They can all be led into delirium, such as in the liquidation of goods in advertising operations such as on days such as "Black Friday".

The cult of the personality is fundamental for mantain the delirium in which the perverse subject remains cohesive. Giving visibility to agents is part of this, because the fascist leader does not survive without external validation. In his delusional narcissism, he needs the show as much as his party. The feeling of inexistence of an authoritarian personality is proportional to its degree of authoritarianism. Narcissus is not only someone who loves himself too much, but also someone who needs a mirror to recognize himself. In its background, there is a subjectivity marked by primitive identification with the "same" and with no place for the "other." To the mass that gives him existence, the

---

[4] Adorno, Theodor. *Aspekte des neuen Rechts-Radikalismus*. Berlin: Suhrkamp, 2019. p. 26.

leader gives the blood or the head of the enemy as in other times. Thus, Trump offers the blood of Mexicans, for example including their children, as once did a Roman emperor. The democratic personalities suffer, the authoritarian ones rejoice, and the perverse leader continues in his place of power.

As an authoritarian personality, the fascist is a priest of conventionalism who practices authoritarianism as religion—and many times religion as authoritarianism—and uses ready-made lines that always converge on the extermination of the other, whoever the other may be.

Authoritarian Thinking Regime

There is no policy without linguistic practices. However, they end up either building and rebuilding or destroying politics. Dialogue generates policy. Hate breaks with dialogue and generates anti-politics. Politics in itself is "dialogue." It should not be reduced to the theater of the power game that we see today, which explains why so many people hate politics. This difference between real politics and power games corresponds to the practice of dialogue, or the absence thereof. In the absence of dialogue and in the advance of the power play, authoritarianism is practically a logical effect. The war of all against all is a power of politics that is only contained if democratic limits are respected.

By authoritarianism we designate an anti-democratic way of exercising power that is expressed in words and deeds. The centrality of authority is the attribute or characteristic of a government, a culture, or even a person exercising authoritarian power. Authoritarianism is the denial of alterity, of the dimension of the "other", in which there is no dialogue because that dimension has been erased. Dialogue and collective participation in decisions are unthinkable in the spectrum of authoritarianism that is defined by the imposition by force of laws of interest to those who exercise power, owners of the means of production of language, goods and capital, exploiters of land and bodies. The other, whether a concrete person, the people, society, other forms of culture or nature, is manipulated in contexts of authoritarianism, when not violated, both physically and symbolically, to serve them.

It is important to realize that behind the authoritarian posture there is a regime of thought. A mental operation that, in a broad sense, becomes paradigmatic acting on the body itself and the dimension of the other. The regime of authoritarian thinking exercises its validity against science, art, culture as a whole and prevails within the scope of common sense.

Authoritarianism as a regime of thought could be overcome by a regime of democratic thought. Not the thought about democracy, but a mental operation, which is, in itself, democratic. In both cases, it is about ways of thinking, and seeing the world and a specific use of language that is effective in actions that affect the world, society, people and nature. The dialogical posture that implies capacity for self-reflection and search for the other, which implies curiosity and the capacity for empathy and compassion, is the way to democracy while sort of a mental functioning.

The operation of authoritarian thinking is deeply rooted in everything we do and seems to strengthen at certain times. It is important to pay attention to this aspect of this operation, namely, the deletion of the "oblative" function (the function of the other) also in relation to time and history. Authoritarian personalities tend to hate history and deny it, while at the same time creating myths related to the past. They also create mystifications and fallacies related to the present in which the other has a function: that of being the enemy who mistreats. Not only the enemy as something undesirable, but in a cunning game of our time, the enemy is transformed in an oppressor. It may sound incredible, but there is a fascist victimization going on. Racists and sexists always complain that they are victims of prejudices created by the anti-racist struggle and by feminists who have, once again, been treated as "witches." All this is part of the advancement of the authoritarian mentality.

The operation of authoritarian thinking is infertile and rigid; it is content to repeat what is given, ready or resolved (even if only apparently). The other (be it the people, or the neighbor, or the culture of the other, or nature or society, or the other as a "voice" that one does not want to hear) is erased in the language process. In this process, the one who has been constituted as an "authoritarian subject" thinks from ready-made statements, from clichés, which are taken as their own, but which are introjected from outside.

In the time of the Internet and especially of social networks with their uninterrupted flow of information, the "copy and paste" type of thinking has become a new type of "method." Descartes was harshly criticized for having spoken of four rules of the method,[5] rules that

---

[5] Descartes, René. Discours de la Méthode. Œuvres complètes, III: Discours de la Méthode/Dioptrique/Météores/La Géométrie. Gallimard, 2009.

seemed to limit the scope of knowledge and restrict the understanding of its production. Today we can say that there are basically two rules at work in the digital society: copy and paste. Thus, with only two movements, there is the digital act that characterizes the way of being and acting in the Internet age.

What does this "copy and paste" method consist of? Talk for talk, no thought for what someone says. Repeat what is said on television (used in less intellectualized cultural classes), on social networks. Sharing content without reading it, which resembles "one-click buying" on the Internet. In all these cases, we act in a vacuum. We are merely reproducing information that means nothing to us who act on its direction. Consumption is just that empty doing. We flee from analytical and critical thinking through the consumerist emptiness of language and repetitive action. We flee from the discernment that analytical and critical thinking demand. We fall into the consumerism of language.

Violence is experienced, provoked and suffered in the daily lives of people in many different ways. In practice, violence is commonplace, i.e., it is common and shared. What we call "symbolic violence"[6] is among us, dangerously intertwined with physical violence. This means that in physical acts of violence of gender, race, age, social class there is always symbolic violence. However, all symbolic violence weighs materially.

Verbal aggression is a known form of symbolic violence. Gossip and defamation are also part of this violence that is carried out using

---

[6] Bourdieu, Pierre. *Le Sens Pratique*, Paris: Édition De Minuit, 1980.

words and acts of speech, but, in most cases, on a scale that does not seem as dangerous. Talking is doing, but we think little about it.

When the violence of speech reaches the communication that, on an institutional scale, reaches the mass media, the danger intensifies. Journalists with ample space on television speak aggressively and irresponsibly using gestures that clearly promote hatred. Extrapolating ethical limits, what television presenters do is to establish links—the affective bonds of which Freud spoke—with the "voice" of many people. This means that prejudices pronounced on the television and computer screens find direct links with those that are pronounced at home, in the sphere of private life. Hence the special place in our contemporary culture of platforms such as Facebook—where anyone can be an "opinion maker"—which has blurred the boundaries between the private and the public. Now what would have been said on a private scale is said on a public scale and becomes politically valid.

But there is continuity between acts of speech and physical violence, because our acts have an effect on what we think. Our acts of speech provoke subjective and objective effects. We may think that we are all capable of gossip, slander and, if well paid, some would even be capable of unethical journalism. How far does the ability to practice violence go? That is a question we must ask ourselves these days.

For example, someone who verbally promotes violence works in the establishment of symbolic violence. The trivialization of violence means that everyone considers themselves authorized to practice it. The various cases of barbaric violence experienced throughout the world in recent times have confronted us with a society that is not concerned with violence itself. The media enters this field controlling people's way of thinking and therefore acting so that they accept violence as something inevitable and, perhaps, even, fun. Evidently, in the condition of message reproducers, each one participates in it. We know that the destruction of society occurs in the destruction of people's subjectivity. There are machines that destroy subjectivities, machines that empty people, they are the devices of the mass media: televisions, computers, cell phones. They are like weapons one should not play with. These are devices that can convert against their own users. In authoritarian regimes everyone must be annihilated as a person. Each one must have lost themselves; in other words, they must give up on themselves in order to be able to feel that the life of the other is not worthwhile and that it must be annihilated in any case. The logic of fascism is pure violence. The authoritarian personality is the one who surrenders to the act of throwing the first stone because it concludes that, from this gesture, it is life can be worth something. There is no future for a society whose common thought is this.

That thought is at the heart of capitalist greed. How to change that state of affairs?

Let us look at the issue of television, which functions as a device of which we are "employees."[7] In many countries around the world, television has replaced books and other forms of communication. The big TV stations are always involved with the coups d'état. Neo-Pentecostal churches buy television and radio networks all over the world. That does not mean that people who watch television do not read books, but it does mean that there is a culture in which

---

[7] Flusser, Vilém. *Filosofia da Caixa Preta*. Rio de Janeiro: Relume Dumará, 2002.

television has such incredible power that it dismisses with other "intellectual" experiences. This is the case in Brazil, a society forged on television, a society abandoned to the screen. Television is an aesthetic and intellectual experience, an experience of knowledge, only highly marked by the impoverishment of language. The computer and cell phone imitate television in its ability to trap the senses on the screen, to produce the same sensory dependence in people as do drugs. That is why reflecting on its role is so fundamental. If the production of personality depends on the means of production of language, in the era of technological means, it is necessary to understand the technologies through which this personality—or this authoritarian subjectivation—is produced. If technical rationality is the rationality of domination,[8] the technical means need to be better understood.

Television operates from the most primitive of our feelings, which is envy. In fact, envy is a posture that opposes the posture of gratitude.[9] Envy is authoritarian while gratitude is democratic. The metaphor of the "glass eye"[10] helps us to explain the place of television as a "prosthesis of knowledge" and, in this sense, a means of de-subjectivation. The object that is a "glass eye" presents us with the structure of envy. It is an eye that devours, while it is an eye that cannot see. Behind the glass eye there is no real sight. It is a blind eye that fits the appearance and works as a visual prosthesis. Television is

---

[8] Adorno, Theodor Wisengrund and Horkheimer, Max. *Dialektik der Aufklärung. Philosophische Fragmente.* In: Adorno, Theodor Wisengrund. *Gesammelte Werke*, Vol. 3. Frankfurt am Main: Suhrkamp, 1997.

[9] Klein, Melanie. *Envy and Gratitude and other works 1946-1963.* Vintage Classics, 1996.

[10] See Tiburi, Marcia. *Olho de Vidro. A televisão e o Estado de Exceção da Imagem.* Rio de Janeiro: Record, 2011.

also a visual prosthesis, which has a purely aesthetic, entertainment function, and a knowledge function that hides its deceptive character.

Hate for Everyone

The irony of authoritarianism is elected by the people. Hate spreads on a systemic level like a fuel for capital. Dialogue would never mean claiming the gaze of the powerful or the executioners who support the suffering of the world, but seeking openness to the other who suffers.

However, "how to talk to fascists" if disruptive and corrosive hatred is given in the posture of the authoritarian personality functioning as fuel for anti-politics? We can ask ourselves the question about the risk of hatred becoming structural, will provide a basis for all our relations in a great war of all against all. However are not we in that war anymore? Whether war is the end of politics or the beginning of it, to stay between Clausewitz and Foucault,[11] does not matter. The fact is that the inevitable relationship between politics and war is a principle of capitalism.

In this context, politics is systematically destroyed in two lines: by the politicians who transform it into bureaucracy; by the people who neglect it and take no interest in it. Those who call themselves non-political, no matter how cynical, win elections in the most diverse

---

[11] Foucault, Michel. *Il faut défendre la société*. Paris: Cours au Collège de France.1976. The French philosopher proposed reversing Clausewitz' classic proposition "War is nothing more than the continuation of politics by other means" to the following formula: "politics is continued war by other means."

countries where democracy has become a simple bureaucracy. Perhaps the destruction of politics is the hidden truth in today's Reason of State. Everyone knows, even if they have no words to express it, that politics has been transformed into bureaucracy and publicity and that governments bureaucratically guarantee their eternal employment by stimulating hatred of public power. What would be "common" to be constructed by all is not an idea conveyed by the media. There is no better way to destroy politics than by making efficient use of hatred.

To destroy the other, it is necessary to destroy politics. To destroy politics, you have to destroy the other. Destroying the other means guaranteeing the end of subjects' rights. This is achieved using processes of humiliation and degradation of people and populations. At the same time, in these contexts it is practical to use the word democracy magically, as if it were already realized.

For now we need to know that affective investments are in idiosyncrasies. The differences in class, race, gender and sexuality, in addition to the pattern of physical normality, are the focus of hateful affection that does not resist without envy and fear. It is necessary to intensify the difference through its own marking to locate a target against which to act in words and deeds. We can thus say that hatred passes between us. However the curious thing is that it does not just happen unconsciously. There is something scary about contemporary hatred. There is no shame in it, it is allowed today, and it is not avoided. The strange authorization for hatred comes from a manipulation not perceived from discourses and devices that create this affection. We are capable of loving and hating. The reason we love is inversely proportional to the reason we hate. In the first case we build, in the second we destroy.

Now, we know that affections are always learned. They form in us by experience. A fascist person is powerless to love because they have lived sensitive and cognitive experiences of hatred. Hate was internalised long before the consciousness could reflect on it. Everything we think is motivated by affective elements. All the thoughts of those who systematically hate are based on the violent power of hatred.

We know that to exterminate the politics is like a rule of capitalism in its savage style the very rich few, the exploited masses and those increasingly sunk in the path of misery so those obediently led. Extermination is calculated: those who do not produce and consume according to the standards of capital have no place. Hatred generates a no place, the space inhabited by the excluded, which is not a political place, but one anti-political in the sense of the negativity of the political being that we naturally are.

The struggle of the excluded is to leave this place gaining a voice and chance to survive. In a truly democratic policy there should be room for everyone, for various modes of production of existence and subsistence which do not need to follow the ordering of capital toward itself, only its own maintenance and reproduction from the devouring of the other.

A substantial, truly theological nucleus of capitalism, the capital is a kind of absolute unity to which everything serves. The violence generated around it to support it has no measures. Barbarism serves capitalism, but is barbarism not the very aesthetic and political expression of capitalism? Could capitalism be anything better than that?

Democracy should be the opposition to this aesthetic and political unity, but it is manipulated in capitalism as if it were that unity itself, which could have happened to us best in socio-political terms. Another democracy, therefore, one that strips itself of its agreement with capital is at stake in a critique of capitalism. A democracy as a break with the games of oppression, domination and exploitation would be the anticipation of a radical democracy. However, the very extermination of the desire for democracy is essential to maintain the system of oppression that we call capitalism, which uses democracy as a mask, a façade. The propaganda of democracy is not democracy.

Machine to Produce Fascists—The Origin and Transmission of Hatred

The social expression of hatred makes us curious as to its origin. We call hate affection that is expressed as intolerance, projective violence or, in the extreme, a declaration of death to the other. We think that someone— one of the many political leaders of our time who remind us of Hitler— pushes the button of hatred that links to the machine producing fascists who make up today's society. This gives the authorization to hate, and even kill, as in the figure of Bolsonaro and similar in Brazil today. The phenomenon of the production of fascist subjectivities implies the potency of the transmissibility of class hatred, race, gender, sexuality, religion, and ethnicity. How to do someone hate? By using speech and propaganda. However why does propaganda lead people to hatred?

It is an organized gear, a kind of device that uses hateful affection to orchestrate the collective delirium to which society itself is relegated. Hate is the opium of the people. The annihilation of a certain idea of society, of the sense of the social, is sustained in the type of fascist subjectivity. The annihilation of politics is the annihilation of the social that needs to be introjected by the concrete individual; someone cancelled as a social being. It would be necessary to unravel the bonds that sustain the delusional hatred in which someone was involved as an individual when they believed that this affection would reside the truth of his experience.

We can define hatred as a passionate emotion. Hence the impression, in the context of its manifestations, that it is a primitive and non-cultural affection, that it is wild and uncivilized. The expression of hatred may seem the irruption of something irrational within a reasonable society. So we tend to see it as something archaic. However, if hatred erupts within civilized society at its technological stage and, in our time, at the height of its digital technological progress, it is because, in some way, it is part of that society in the form of a dominant rationality.

The question of the origin of hatred can only be answered by resorting to the vicious circle that explains the appearance of any affection. We are affected by collectively experienced feelings, in other words, experiences with personal inferiority are the result of external inputs. This means that the tendency to see affection as something particular and natural loses sight of the social character of its constitution. Affections are learned, are shared among people through speeches, images and narratives. Affections are part of processes of cognition and subjective formation. Someone who has experienced love responds with love, someone who has experienced hatred responds with hatred. Loving learns love. Hate I learn by hating.

In this way, we cannot speak of the chronological origin of affection. Hate is not implanted as a "chip" in a person nor is it explained by a naturally "hateful personality" as opposed to a naturally "loving personality." Understanding hatred becomes possible if we pay attention to the genealogical character of the experience of hatred. It happens every time we let ourselves be affected by it, in the same way that we let ourselves be affected by love. Hatred is not something that is present in some people as opposed to others, but is something that is a shared experience with others. "How can anyone be taken by hatred?" is a question that help us to understand the character proper to emotions, that of being strangely contagious.

When we talk about affection, we talk about what "touches us," what concerns us. What "touches us" refers to what is somehow perceived, by being communicated, by being transmitted. It is what is shared, but not just from "top to bottom," as if, in the case of hatred, we had received an order, conscious or unconscious, to feel it and express ourselves in its name. It is necessary to respond positively to what comes from above and make it horizontal.

If we think of the speeches of incitement to violence—one of the expressive forms of hatred—we see that it is transmitted from the top down, as in a gear driven from the outside. Political, advertising, journalistic, and religious leaders, and all those who can producing this discourse can connect to this machine by inciting hatred. But the "vertical" element that connects the machine moved by hatred is not enough to sustain it, so in order for it to persist, its experience must be affirmed "horizontally," that is, it must be shared with peers, with others who contribute to the maintenance of the machine which by fostering hatred of the other, transforms everyone into fascists. Fascism is the hatred-driven machine which produces an ever-increasing number of fascists.

Thus, each one can become a gear in the great machine to produce fascists fed with the fuel of hatred. It would only be possible to stop if one learns that there is another way.

Love and hatred are opposing forces, while at the same time they go together. Sometimes they get too close. They are like two lines that tend to curl up while floating in the historic wind. We think of the "chronology," of progress and decadence, but we reflect little on the affections that sew and neglect the continuum of history. Now, we could write the history of love and hatred considering that there is no historical period in which they have not featured. It would be the story of affective influences on human actions and accomplishments. So, for example, we could tell the story of the relationship between humanity and nature by thinking about how the former hated the latter. The proof is that nature is being destroyed.

The waves of love and hatred that sustain and shake societies cannot be controlled simply, but can be manipulated. This control is possible through language because it is the great producer of affections. Through mechanisms that only may seem subtle to those who remain naive, hatred is fomented on a social scale by the bombing of terrible images, such as those we see on television. The distortion of facts to convince the people is also linked to this strategy of manipulation of affections through speeches. At the origin of all hatred is the basic slander that, on a professional scale, comes to create the universe of Fake News.

In very simple terms, we can say that love is a horizon of understanding that takes into account the real dimension of the other, that does not invent it in a projection, that remains open to its mystery.

If love is open to the other, hate is closed to it. We tend not to want to see the hatred that closes us in because it diminishes us. "Not wanting to see" is a trap, because we are all affected by hatred and we all contribute to its persistence.

When we talk about affection, we mean that something "affects" us, that it provokes us. Hate takes the form of a miasma, that is, an atmosphere. It exists as an air we can breathe. You feel things that you might never have felt. However, hatred is not a feeling that would be kept within us, waiting to appear but an experience that is possible in every moment we have with the other who affects us. In this general framework, asking about the state of the affective experience of hatred in our innermost parts can be a way to start getting rid of it.

Language Consumerism

Authoritarianism is a regime of thought that affects knowledge. It is not only established in ethical–political terms, but also in aesthetic terms. This means, in the personal formation of social relations, but also of a way of life developed in terms of a style of living that is destructive and capable of covering up its own destruction.

In this sense, we can speak of a regime of democratic thought that is essentially opposed to the regime of authoritarian thought. As a worldview, authoritarianism is closed. It operates through discourse and practice that are organized in the manner of a great fallacy in which thought is, in fact, the production of absence or, to use Hannah

Arendt's famous expression, a "void of thought".[12] Authoritarian thinking fights the freedom and expressiveness of thought.

This is achieved by fostering the cliché, by maintaining and repeating ready-made thinking, which we can also call "advertising thinking". In the latter, seductive and unquestionable certainties are presented. Advertising thinking aims to bring consumers together using ready-made ideas. Language consumption is the goal of enterprises that produces language. Entertainment is an industry and market of language. Thus, everything is language for consumption: film, fashion, body, architecture, art and even philosophy.

The scope of truth (as a desire for unveiling) is something that is further outside the reach of advertising power, than it would be an order of advertising discourse. The same happens in the field of action that we can call "pseudo-action," the repetitive action, and the pre-programmed action, such as that of consumerism.

Thought and action are linked and organized in a complex theoretical–practical imperative, therefore, an obligatory way of thinking and acting, of high-performative impact: the other does not exist and if it does, it must be eliminated, to pass from its condition of "anybody," "nobody." Let us recall here the chapter of the Dialectics of the Enlightenment of Adorno and Horkheimer in which the authors analyze the meeting of Ulysses and the Cyclops Polyphemus[13] to think

---

[12] Arendt, Hannah. *Eichmann in Jerusalem*. Penguin, 2006.

[13] Adorno, Theodor Wisengrund and Horkheimer, Max. *Dialektik der Aufklärung. Philosophische Fragmente*. In: Adorno, Theodor Wisengrund. *Gesammelte Werke*, Vol. 3. Frankfurt am Main: Suhrkamp, 1997. Ulysses says to Polypheme: "*My name is Nobody!*" 'When, drunk and wounded, the Cyclops call his friends, he'll explain:' *Nobody hurt me!* 'His brethren will answer:' *Then pray to the gods, for there is nothing to do.*"

about how language is distorted or used cunningly to annihilate the other. The chapter examines how Ulysses uses his cunning to escape from Polyphemus, who devoured his fellow travelers and intended to do the same with him. Ulysses deceives Polyphemus by saying his own name, Odysseus. It turns out that his name sounds like "Oudeis," which means "No one" and Ulysses does it on purpose to deceive the Cyclops and pierce his only eye. By saying "my name is Nobody," Ulysses denies his own identity, but deceives the giant and manages to hang under the belly of a sheep while it is caressed by the cyclops, a primitive and half silly being. Upon entering the ship, already safe from the wounded giant, he cannot stand to keep the secret and shouts out his true name explaining to the giant what he did. Nonetheless he confesses because he feared he would lose himself by losing his identity. Ulysses is, according to the authors of the Dialectics of the Enlightenment, the prototype of the bourgeois individual who needs to laugh at, humiliate and demean the other to sustain his identity. It is not yet the authoritarian fascist who destroys everything, but there is within him the same seed of instrumental rationality that, according to Frankfurt's philosophers, will lead to fascism.

To reduce the other to "no one," to erase the identity of the other would be the only way to preserve one's own identity? Ulysses reduces language according to his needs. Is it the principle of epistemological violence that, in this scene of the *Odyssey*, governs this encounter between the "bourgeois" and the non-bourgeois that exists until today?

Now, what does advertising do but reduce people and citizens to "nobody"? Advertising uses the principle of humiliation against people, each one is humiliated in the condition of an infantilized citizen, naive, incapable of perceiving the rhetorical game of which someone is a victim. What does neoliberalism—and machismo and sexism, and homophobia, and racism—do but erase the other in the right to be who someone is? Could these postures—or impostures—survive without their eternal propaganda?

Reductionism occurs through verbal and non-verbal acts, but also through acts related to the production of images. The consumerism of language is the effect of a society in which the image has become capital and words have no value as means of reflection. It is the communication itself that is annihilated.

One of the features of today's culture is the proliferation of texts, ideas and opinions. Sharing private information has become a compulsive gesture since the invention of the Internet and, even more so, of social networks. We can say that today we live in the excesses of language, proliferating and replicating everything that appears before us. If, as Wittgenstein said, the limits of the world are the limits of my language, then there are people who must believe that, by quantity, we have become great people living in very vast worlds.

There are not always criteria in the performance of our acts of language. We talk a lot and think little about what we say. On the one hand, we may be thinking too fast, on the other hand, we may be relying too much on the ready-made thoughts that are served to us until we find more careful thoughts. In the midst of language in which we entangle ourselves, we lose the chance to understand why we pick the first explanation in the marketplace of ideas that appear to us exposed on a shelf of offers.

We keep leaving aside the potential to understand. What is explained already serves us well. Meanwhile, in the democracy of affections, suffering is being shared among us. Like all anguish, it does not have a definite face. An anguish that contaminates everything that is said without being able to know exactly what it means. It is not uncommon to feel that, amidst so much that has already been said and is still being said, there is not much more to be said and that, for this very reason, one should try to say something new. Or shut up for good. Sliding on one's own intention and saying "anything" is, however, much easier. There is a pleasure in speaking that cannot be compared to the pleasure of shutting up. It is clear that in a society in which pleasures are controlled and administered, speech, not silence, is encouraged. Noise serves many things, especially the generation of a void of thought.

Producing the emptiness of thought, and the emptiness of one's own emotions that lead to empty lines in oneself, is part of the project of today's society. It is complicated to say "project of society" because society, this self-organized whole, seems exactly not projected and sustained in a vacuum. The will to speak without having anything to say is a portrait of how we are socially lost in this collectivized and democratized void. Capitalism produces vacuity for everyone. We feel lost in a great mismatch orchestrated by the technical rationality that is the rationality of domination.

In this general emptiness we do not know who to speak to. We talk to ourselves on social networks, waiting for someone to read and validate us. This lack of place combined with the compulsion to say generates disasters. The affections that build a chaotic climate are the same that led to an odious climate among us today. Widespread hate speech in the disinformation and defamation industry is used against specific targets, but much is said without a destination address. On social networks, people are able to engage with those who embrace this type of hate speech.

The subject of hate speech can be chauvinism, may be racism, homophobic, and can even be xenophobic. Words become weapons. Prejudice is a type of injustice practiced in language, also created through it to the extreme of crimes. It is in this sense that we can say that to speak is to do something severe. However, the habit of practicing prejudiced discursive acts poses another problem besides the violation of laws. A culture of violent and prejudiced acts of speech destroys the spirit, critical thinking, and ethics that result from it.

If we take into account that saying something is very easy, that we talk too much and that we say unnecessary things, that we compulsively send and repeat messages, a new consumerism emerges among us: the consumerism of language. The problem is that this produces, like any consumerism, a lot of garbage. The problem is that this profoundly alters our lives in a physical and mental sense. What one eats, what one sees, what one hears, in a word, what one introjects, becomes body, and becomes existence.

Paranoia and Ecstasy

The authoritative subject, in a broad sense, is a paranoid guy. In *Totem and Taboo*,[14] comparing records and fields of human production, Freud will say that hysteria is like a work of art, just as obsessive neurosis is like a religion. Regarding the idea of a system, Freud approached

---

[14] Freud, Sigmund. *Totem und Tabu*. Fischer, 2013.

paranoia and philosophy. However while culture is the excellence of human spiritual production, disease is its failure. This explains the success that certain charlatans make today in Brazilian culture, using the word "philosophy" to regiment armies of people affected by the paranoid condition. Paranoia implies a delirium, but because of its scope, it is now a condition. Absolutely devoid of any of its historical or current senses, the word philosophy used by certain characters who call themselves philosophers, could be replaced simply by "paranoia."

For Freud, paranoia is a type of defense, that is, a type of disorder linked to representation in the early stages of the formation of the subject in childhood. In paranoia something is denied due to its unbearable character. In this case, homosexuality understood as an inevitable and forbidden identification which cannot appear under risk of destroying the subject of paranoia. The mechanism of repression implies throwing away, psychically speaking, the unbearable content. Nevertheless one cannot erase the subjective story that accumulates at an unconscious level. It returns. It is in this scenario that is situated the famous case of Schreber's fantasy, a character about which Freud wrote one of his most important studies.[15] Schreber became convinced that he could save the world, but this could only be achieved if he was transformed into a woman, creating a new population after being impregnated by God. God, in this case, represents everything that was badly solved in the prehistory of subjective life. Schreber's paranoia is still alive among us, in the era of authoritarian neo-Pentecostalism.

It is not by chance that God returns to the fore today in the contemporary fascisms promoted by neo-fundamentalist churches.

---

[15] Freud, Sigmund. *The Schreber Case*. London: Penguim, 2003.

We have just witnessed a coup d'état in Bolivia in which the local white bourgeoisie (which is not white on the racist scale of the world) overthrew Evo Morales, an indigenous man who had been democratically elected for his third term. We can call the economic and ideological class that holds world money the "ultra-bourgeoisie" and the bourgeoisie "medio bourgeoisie" who enforce the coups carried out by the corporations who serve capital. The various social classes are engaged in the ideological process (theoretical and practical) that leads to the coups. Their goal is always power.

The participation of the neo-Pentecostal sectors in the coup against Evo Morales was evident. God has played an important role as a means to justify paranoid religion and bourgeoisie. However, we must ask ourselves, what allows people to engage in the paranoid dimension? There is the construction of a scene that has the objective of realizing catharsis in whoever is captured by it. The function of catharsis in church and in contemporary politics (institutions that are increasingly confused in Brazil and Latin America) is no longer the traditional act of purification, but ecstasy.

Ecstasy is what is achieved in the moment of an immediate emotional bond. It is ecstasy that allows the "psycho-theological" and also the "theo-physiological" bond.[16] It is the emotion found in the marches, at football, and at musical festivals that allows the feeling of belonging. The church provides that for the poor. The desire to be part of an audience—that keeps people in front of television and that is manipulated in cinema today—would also be a religious version of this tactic of capitalism that should not say its name so as not to break

---

[16] Türcke, Christoph. *Sociedade Excitada*. Unicamp, 2010.

the spell. Ecstasy is the feeling of bonding with something transcendental in a world without God, but full of cell phones ensuring "total connection" at all times. The cell phone is a religious organ today and the Internet is the only possible transcendence.

Therefore, churches have been using this feeling of ecstasy for a long time, at least since the Baroque period.[17] From the charismatic movement of the Catholic Church to the exorcism ceremonies of the Brazilian neo-Pentecostal churches spread around the world as multinational companies, what we see is ecstasy. Neoliberalism promises ecstasy for merchandise. It is no coincidence that the name of a synthetic drug that is very common among young people today is "Ecstasy."

Why do the indigenous people manage to remain faithful to Evo Morales and not succumb to a woman who proclaims herself as president? Because there are different gods at stake. God's strategic place in political action is what returns. In Bolivia's coup d'état we see the absence of a pact between groups that have been at war since the beginning of the invasions and the attempt by the economic elites to once again massacre the indigenous people as they did five centuries ago. The Church continues to use the same old tactic: it uses God to provoke the ecstasy of the fascist masses. However not all the masses get carried away.

A paranoid subject, no matter what place it occupies in the system of power that unites everyone, has a kind of pride about his thoughts, as if they were theological truths that he alone holds. That is what we

---

[17] Let us remember the sculpture called The Ecstasy of St. Teresa (c. 1650) of Bernini that presents precisely this spirit between the erotic and the theological.

see with Schreber. His "psychological–theological" system involved a complex power plot between family members and a fantasy solution in the figure of God.

Self-pride, a pathological narcissism that defines the way of being of paranoid subjects, becomes collective in fascism. It is no longer just the pride of an idea, but the pride of being part of a whole. Social networks are spaces in which paranoia can be freely expressed precisely because there is room for it. It is necessary within the system, which it underpins.

In the virtual world, creating an immediate link and achieving different levels of ecstasy is very easy. Between them each one allows the system of power to be constructed. Every authoritarian person feels like a half priest of some cause and feels free to affirm this publicly, especially if that cause is God, or what is confused with him: Capital.

Authoritarian lines are like shattered sentences—or clichés— forcibly glued together to form an image of the world around them. They have the pretension of objectivity, of presenting something that in the fiction of the authoritarian, is already known.

The actual operation of the knowledge that is given to the novelty of the object is unnecessary in the perspective of the authoritarian thought regime of a paranoid. In other words, we can say that the authoritarian subject "asks" and "answers" himself from a previously organized point of view from which, at each moment, the other needs to be discarded. The other is what is recalculated in individual and collective paranoia. As if there were no "other" point of view, another desire, another way of seeing the world, another religion or another football team, what is erased is the "other" that comes to activate the system of fear. Faced with a system in which truths are given, research and investigation, or the simple gesture of reading a book or listening to a person is impossible. Dialogue is a linguistic operation—affective/mental—that implies the other, but it is impossible for a paranoid because, in the extreme, the paranoid knows beforehand what everyone thinks therefore everyone becomes predictable.

Cognitive Deficiency

We perform a mental operation related to the other when we talk about knowledge. This is because knowledge is a cognitive gesture toward the other, the new, and the different, in a word, the unknown. Authoritarianism invents the other in order to be able to make use of it and also destroy it. In this sense, what we call knowledge does not actually happen in the regime of authoritarian thinking. In it, knowledge is a faceless mask. What we call ideology, the overshadowing of undesirable social truths, is directly related to this process of masking through the invention of another to be hated. A projection operation is in progress in the construction of the enemies.

Knowledge cannot be conceived outside its ethical–political record. If the register of knowledge works by denying "the other", it is denial of oneself. Strictly speaking, it is not knowledge. Without the other, knowledge dies, becoming instead ideological blindness. Ideology is the reduction of knowledge to the façade becoming its mortuary mask. Knowledge, which should be a process of encounter and disposition for the otherness that represents it, succumbs to its negation. Hence the impression that we have that an authoritarian personality is also dumb,[18] because it cannot understand the other and anything that is in its orbit.

The field of the other is not accessible to the authoritarian personality because it has no cognitive conditions for this. That means there is a problem with the faculty of understanding. But cognition is not an isolated ability in the mind. Cognition's bodily, environmental, connects to our body. An authoritarian personality, a potential fascist, lacks the affectivity and imagination by which we can approach this field whose epicenter is, in it, always inaccessible. This means that we will never be able to know the "other" as a whole, which would also be an illusory perspective, but that we can have a posture of openness, of curiosity toward the other, of acceptance of the other's difference.

If we think about the other as a spectrum is because it is not rigid, it is a system of representations made up of juxtaposed images, levels and categories. So I can relate to the idea of the other, the image of the other, and the body of the other. To think of the other, for or against it, derives, therefore, from the affection that presides over the thought.

---

[18] Stupidity is not a despicable category, but a philosophical theme linked to the field of morality and psychology, a discipline that arises from questions raised in the field of philosophy. Stupidity becomes an issue in authors such as Kant in his Essay on Mental Illness, in Musil, in the Essay on Stupidity, in Nietzsche and in Adorno and Horkheimer's Dialectics of Enlightenment. See Robert Musil's 1937 conference entitled "Über die Dummheit". (*From Stupidity*. Manuel Alberto. Lisbon: Water Clock, 1994.) See also: Nietzsche, Friedrich. *Über Warheit und Lüge im Aussermoralischen Sinn*. Werke in drei Bänden. München: Carl Hanser, 1973. p. 309.

Propaganda is the method that sustains the denial of the other. Fascist propaganda, the propaganda of hatred, preaches intolerance, affirms terrible things with high performative content, which is, capable of provoking effects and guiding actions. What I call advertising here is not the advertising campaign, but rather the discursiveness rooted in the most common speeches and the harmful speeches of power. In everyday life, especially in certain moments of crisis of capitalism, we see the hyperactivity of propaganda that tries to maintain the cohesion of a broken system. All the presidents of countries whose democracies have died by shock rhetoric.

Today, when I rewrite this book and remember examples such as that of a deputy from the south of Brazil, a part of the country colonized by Italy and Germany, named Luis Carlos Heinze who presented, in a speech that can still be seen on YouTube, a perfect image of authoritarian thinking that excludes the other, I think that, unfortunately, since the first edition of this book was published, everything has become worse. I cite this Brazilian example, but at the same time, it has some European connection, because Heinze is a descendant of Germans who lived in southern Brazil, which was colonized by Germans in the nineteenth century. The south of Brazil reflected many of the racist ideologies present in Europe at that time. Of course, racist prejudice persists and is renewed.

In his speech, which became famous, "quilombolas, Indians, gays, lesbians," represented "Tudo o que não presta." "All who don't matter" is undoubtedly a way to disqualify others, just as the German Nazis did with the undesirables of their time: Jews, people with disabilities, people of other ethnicities. "All who don't matter" is the exact opposite of statements like "Black Lives Matter". In this case, the subjects disqualified in Heinze speech were the historically oppressed political minorities in the capitalist system. Political minorities created by capitalism as the "blacks" who form the only human beings to have their flesh and their skin transformed into merchandise[19] were people kidnapped in Africa and taken to the Americas. In an act of extreme racism, Bolsonaro once asked how many "arrobas" have people living in the Quilombos? Quilombos are areas populated largely by the descendants of slaves; and the term "arroba" defined the load that a donkey or mule could carry.

With the expression "All who don't matter," the aforementioned Brazilian deputy declared the fundamental concept of current fascism: "All who don't matter " implies a downgrading of the people indicated in his speech. It is "no matter" for the production and consumption system.

The fascist discourse, on the other hand, as the quintessence of the authoritarian personality, is one that imposes the point of view of the judgment of the other for its possible utility. The logic of the measure and the reification is what is on the scene. The fascist is the priest of capitalism whose liturgy implies this judgment, like a perverse baptism: the other is discarded and abandoned and, in the extreme, into death, as we see happening in the genocide of black youth and children in Rio. It is the destruction of the very idea of human dignity that we are witnessing.

"All who don't matter" at the same time presents itself as a ready-made answer, a cliché. An example of the destruction of knowledge as

---

[19] Mbembe, Achille. *Critique de la raison nègre*. La Découverte, 2013.

a desire for discovery, which constitutes the relationship with the other in its condition of being different, an image of the otherness to be respected. Desire for knowledge that underlies desire for democracy. The expression is a self-assertion of ignorance, a signature of stupidity. At the same time, it is the destruction of politics by an anti-political discourse of an agent of government which should be political, but instead is focused on anti-political death. Examples around the world are not lacking in figures that frighten us when they speak in this way.

In a case like this, the practice of discourse is dangerous and threatening. The tendency to exterminate is part of it. "Matability," or "the character of being exposed to killing," is created by the "tanatopolitics" of our time. Tyrants boast about it. Foucault, in his history of sexuality, will speak of tanatopolitics and biopolitics to define a change of political regimes concerning life. Tanatopolitics is the policy of death. Biopower means the calculation that power makes over life. Biopower is the typical way of exercising power in modern times, when it is no longer a matter of simply condemning to death, as in antiquity. In modernity, "biopower" is the calculation of life. It acts as an example, controlling the prices and distribution of food, access to health care, places of residence, work, and the remuneration of populations. Exclusion is the process guaranteed by the precariousness to which many people are condemned.

Mortality due to lack of public policies and a radically democratic project in the country is always a guaranteed result. If the State does not serve the people, it serves the elites. The "tanato-pouvoir" continues to act through biopower: calculating life to cast into death those who are marked with the iron of uselessness.

The uselessness of people and their disposability must be guaranteed epistemologically, which is achieved through the discourse that is part of the order. However, who is convinced by this kind of discourse? This is a question we have to ask ourselves, namely if we are to be able to combat these forms of discourse or create alternatives for the survival of a democratic policy, for a better policy, for a power that becomes a power of difference, a power of understanding that embraces what Walter Benjamin called the "tradition of the oppressed." Now, those who speak in defense of prejudice and incitement to violence, on the one hand, must be questioned legally. On the other hand, it is necessary to understand the conditions in the culture that make it possible to make statements which allow disqualification of the other and their differences. Why do people accept and repeat fascist hate speech?

Theodor Adorno asked how people become susceptible to fascist propaganda.[20] Who is, after all, susceptible to propaganda in general and susceptible to fascist propaganda? If fascist propaganda, which is a type of discourse—and a true methodology of social alienation through language—continues to win, we will have no future. And this is not an issue that should be forgotten, although many might prefer that the theory remains pure analytical that stops us from pointing this path. A projective question imposes itself philosophically at this moment: in what way should we act before this state of affairs takes

---

[20] Adorno, Theodor. "Education After Auschwitz," *Critical Models: Interventions and Catchwords*, trans. Henry W. Pickford. New York: Columbia University Press, 2005.

hold? But we still need to look more at the social bases of the problem we have to solve.

On Emptiness: Thinking, Feeling, Acting and the Lack Thereof

We can characterize our time from three great voids.

The first of them is the void of thought. Hannah Arendt was the thinker responsible for her formulation in a book called *Eichmann in Jerusalem*[21] in which she gives a philosophical account of the trial of a high-ranking official of the German Nazi regime who, however, was not one of her main mentors. Adolf Eichmann, who was captured in Argentina and tried in Jerusalem for his crimes against humanity, appalled the world by presenting himself as a citizen like any other who intended only to advance in his career by claiming to follow orders. In the book, she says that Eichmann did not show that he was reflecting on what he had done as an employee. It is like his ability to think had been interrupted. When questioned, Eichmann answered using clichés and, at the same time, he was not a perverse subject who was using some kind of intelligence to do evil consciously.

It was by analyzing the figure of Eichmann that Arendt launched the question of the emptiness of thought. The characteristic of this form of emptiness is the absence of reflection, of criticism, of questioning and even of discernment. We can say that, in our time,

---

[21] Arendt, Hannah. *Eichmann in Jerusalem*. Penguin, 2006.

this is becoming more and more common. More and more people are giving up the ability to think. However, it seems absurd that we can live without thought which is exactly why the use of ready-made ideas has become more and more functional every day, as was already the case with Eichmann. Today, social networks survive mainly through the flow of ready-made ideas. People become every day transmitters of unquestioned ideas. Ideas that are like takeaway goods without asking what meaning they can have in the life of those who take them with them.

In the field of propaganda, professionals specialize in presenting rarefied ideas, not only as superficial things, but also as something that is easily available, something whose complexity no longer matters. The ideas themselves are consumed. There is a true consumerism of things, but also of ideas and, in that sense, also of the language through which they circulate. Now, the status of things in a world focused on hyper-consumption is that of being disposable. *Are ideas now as disposable as the next consumable things?* Or would the ideas only serve to give an "aura" to these things that, in themselves, don't have? I think here of the idea of "personal merit" which generates a culture of "meritocracy," for example, through which historical and social conditions are hidden, as well as prejudices of race, gender and class—which are part of a person's "victories and defeats." Even the concepts of "victory" and "defeat" are not questioned by people in the context of common sense.

From this we can speak of a second form of emptiness that characterizes our world that is increasingly in need of examination. This is about how we feel. We live in a world that is increasingly anesthetized, in which people become incapable of feeling and increasingly insensitive. The society in which we live seems more and more excited, anguished and doomed to despair. We can speak of an emptiness of emotion precisely in the context in which people seek, any kind of emotion. It is expensive to pay for the lack of feelings that we can define, in a generic sense, as a generalized coldness. The inability to feel makes the field of sensitivity in us a place of despair. From joy to sadness, we want religion, sex, films, drugs, radical sports, and even food to provoke more than feelings. Ecstasy is desired. Emotion has also become a commodity and what does not radically thrill does not seem worth the effort. Hate is a fundamental emotion in our time. For those who can't feel anything, it presents as a strange redemption.

In this context, the goods arise with the promise of ensuring ecstasy. It is hoped today that human experiences will always be more and more intense, cinematic, impressive and spectacular even if it is just some new clothes, a cell phone, a toy or a place to eat, everything is sold as if it were not only what it really is. It is the empire of emotion against boredom, of excitement against boredom, of speed against the natural rhythm of things, of festivity against tranquility, of drunkenness against sobriety.

Now, when we talk about emotions, we tend to think that they are spontaneous. But nothing is really spontaneous in a society that is led by advertising. All this is counterbalanced by the programming of thinking and feeling. And the issue at stake is that of affective emptying in a scenario of human coldness and hysterical expression. But if people are getting colder and colder, it also means that they are necessarily becoming more and more "robotized" by programmed thoughts and feelings.

That is where we can talk about a third void. The emptiness of the action that results from the previously exposed forms of emptying. The loss of a sense of ethics and politics in which human actions have flourished as meaningful activities is evident today. The rise of prejudiced postures in the field of common sense where ethics should thrive and of tyrannical and fascist postures in politics as we see in the authoritarian states that come into being again on a global scale, is one of its results. The emptiness of action is configured as an extirpation of the moral sense that would lead us to act in the common good and with respect for the fundamental rights of human beings for a just life in society.

At the same time, human beings are those who seek to fill their gaps. The emptiness of action gives way to consumerism in which production has a servile and purely utilitarian meaning. But human action always asks to be an invention of life. And it is this invention of life that is emptied by capitalism precisely because capitalism is associated with a deep instinct for death.[22] Destruction and death is the spirit of capitalism organized around suffering, guilt and hatred.

Thoughts and emotions depend on exercises in language environments. We learn to think and feel in contexts such as family, school, work and in the world of life in general. To this plan it is necessary to add social networks that tend to change patterns of thought, emotion and action.

It is in these spaces that we also learn to value what we do when others can recognize us because we also act for them. And this includes

---

[22] Maris, Bernard and Dostaller, Gilles. *Capitalisme et Pulsion de Mort*. Albin Michel, 2009.

linguistic action, which today suffers from the same evil as action in general. Unfortunately, the emptying of linguistic action is seen, above all, in social networks, places where many people speak without having anything to say.

Real life is replaced by virtual life that deludes us that we are not in a desert without knowing what it means to be in a desert.

Cultural Industry of Anti-Politics—The Manipulative Character

In the desert in which we live emptied of subjectivity, proliferate discourses and manifestations of the "manipulative character," a term that appears in various texts of Theodor Adorno to mean objectifying individuals of themselves and others.[23] They are a fundamental part of the anti-politics of our time. Politics is the human capacity to create common bonds in the name of peaceful coexistence among all, which requires the defense of rights for all and respect for each one. Anti-politics, in turn, is the orchestrated destruction of these potentials on an industrial scale, such as the creation of a habitus, a biopolitics and an anatomopolitics. Anti-politics is the name we give to the cultural industry of politics, that is, to politics leached by the rationality of advetsing.

It is important to bear in mind that the struggle for the defense of rights in any society is part of the scenario of valuing both the common and the singular that flourishes in it. What we call common requires the uniqueness that is, at the same time, the function of the

---

[23] "Education after Auschwitz." Op. cit.

"other" as an essential dimension in the life of each one. Now, the common—what we build among ourselves in political terms—is made of singularity and otherness. The common is not simply the collective, because anti-politics also implies something collective.

The difference between masses and multitude interests us. While the masses are amorphous and can be manipulated, the multitude is made up of singularities who express themselves politically in search of a commonality of purpose. To use the above distinction, the multitudes are political; the masses are anti-political. The multitude is the union of singularities, the masses, the meeting of individualities. Multitude preserves the otherness; masses annihilate the uniqueness. Masses are manipulated while the multitude cannot. Mass is authoritarian; multitude is emancipated. Mass is regressive; multitude is progressive. Mass needs a leader to lead it; multitude only needs the desire of each one.

Now, the manipulative character can be a person, a leader, or a group that leads the mass. The manipulative character can be the logic of an institution, of a company, or of a small group such as a "pack."[24] The manipulative character can invade masses, but it cannot dominate multitudes. Sometimes, crowds of people can contain both formations.

It is true that crowds have occupied the streets since 2011 around the world in the so-called "Colour Revolutions," and in Brazil since June 2013. However, an interesting phenomenon needs to be taken into account. Considering the difference between union and meeting, between common and collective, we can say that the demonstrations in the streets were a mixture of mass and crowd.

---

[24] Canetti, Elias. *Mass and power* [Masse und macht]. Farrar, Straus and Giroux, 1984.

It is precisely because of this hybrid character that its appearance is explained. What, in the case of the multitudes, would refer to the sublime grandeur and therefore be something impressive; in the case of the masses would refer to a terrifying monstrosity, as we saw in fascist manifestations on the avenues of some large cities such as São Paulo in 2015 always reported by hegemonic media, as the only crowds on the streets. Today (2019), as I rewrite this book, the crowds are on the streets in Catalonia in the struggle against Spanish authoritarianism and the growth of the extreme right in that country, the Gilets Jeunes take to the streets of Paris, the indigenous and poor people of Bolivia revolt against the bloody, neoliberal and neo-fundamentalist coup, which annihilated democracy in that country. More recently, the multitude were on the streets defending education in Brazil and the right to abortion in Argentina.

The political manifestation depends very much on the desire of the crowd in relation to education, for example. Anti-political demonstration depend on manipulative leaders, presidents or deputies, torturers, television presenters, false pastors, policemen, intellectuals, journalists, judges and a show-making machine. The most diverse characters are seen in this role nowadays.

It is the manipulative character that operates in the formation of the masses, we know this since Gustav Le Bon created the "psychology of the masses" that, as Adorno realized, are instigated by fascist agitators to act in a violent way.[25] The means of discourse production, including the media, have a fundamental role in this process: the

---

[25] Adorno, Theodor. *Die Freudische Theorie und die Struktur der fascistichen Propaganda.* Gesammelte Schriften Vol. 8, T. I [Soziologische Schriften]: Surhkamp Verlag, 1975.

disguised propaganda of journalism cannot hide its fascism, it can transform the fascist worldview (of hatred and denial of otherness) into a value that is praised by those who have never thought in ethical-political terms and, for this very reason, fall into the anti-political trap. Politicians and judicial agents join them in the process of leading the masses.

All institutions assume a manipulative character in moments of fascist ascension. The fascist movement works as a wave that invades and floods all the shores. Thus, in the wreck of society, everyone looks for a piece of the broken boat to grab onto. Political illiterates quickly cling to fascist promises of redemption that offer them prejudices as a lifeline.

If we think of anti-political figures such as homophobic representatives who make homophobia their delirious flag, or other scammers who, with government power in their hands, propose all forms of social regression, we should be very worried, because fascist leaders manipulate the masses inside or outside the governments of the world are proliferating. They are manipulative characters created and, themselves, manipulated by the media, but who, in turn, have a vast experience to offer to these same media that manipulate them. The cynical agreement between these manipulative individuals and the institutions.

These manipulative individuals are not autonomous, they are parts of a machine that sells them as heroes and, in a corrupt way, they use it. They are the corrupt in a corrupting system. Seeing them in action, we might think that the "manipulative character" would be old men, forged by the cold and violent education of the military dictatorship. What about young people who speak in a fascist way? Will manipulated young people, used by the cultural industry of anti-politics led to action by businessmen and sponsors, know what they say? Now, to manipulate young people and children is the most perverse thing, because it is a manipulation that operates on those who have no way to defend themselves. On the other hand, this manipulation implies the death of hope for the future symbolized by young people and children.

Cultural Semi-Forming

There is a text by Theodor Adorno called "Semiculture Theory"[26] or "Semi-formation Theory" in which he speaks of the importance of discernment. The original term for "semi-forming" is "Halbbildung." If "Bildung" refers to cultural education in an extra-pedagogical sense, i.e., not dependent on school education, "semi-forming" would be a precarious, partial way of subjectively appropriating culture. The omnipresence of the alienated spirit and what Adorno called "dissociated consciousness," the inability to establish a link between the learned culture and the purposes for which it is intended, the human issues, concern semi-forming.

When we ask ourselves how it is possible that in the middle of the twenty-first century, at a time when access to information is increasingly widespread, when we have reached a cultural stage— including with digital technology—as impressive as it is possible for

---

[26] Adorno, Theodor. *Theorie der Halbbildung*. Suhrkamp, 2006.

people to talk so much nonsense, we are facing the issue of semi-culture. "Semi-cult" would not only be the almost-formed person, half formed or formed by half, or even badly formed. What is at stake in semi-forming is cognitive rupture. The cognitive gap between what someone learns and what they think and do. The question is certainly in the means of formation, in the unconscious cultural mediations that weigh on us, and in the love–hate that exists towards art and knowledge, as well as towards culture in a fascist society.

Among the Nazis, for example, it was common to value art (not the modern art that Hitler called "degenerate") and feel contempt for humanity. They didn't realize that art was not only an aesthetic issue—in fact, Nazi art was terrible in this sense—but also ethical and political.

The question of the introjection of culture concerns the extra-pedagogical data that form us, that enter our lives, making us who we are. Culture is every kind of experience with music, with every kind of text, art, festive habit, food, social, political, every religious habit, every kind of speech, every kind of experience with the language in its various expressions.

The term "Bildung" has the meaning of construction. It refers to education in the broad sense, not just school education, but education to which we are linked throughout our lives from birth to death. The school institution associated with the market education to merchandise. It reduces people to producers and consumers who should only fit into a market. The creative dimension of life, including economic life, which is the one that most frightens the common sense that can see in education the scope of only one vacancy in a system, is left aside. Moreover, the cultural industry under which we form our current perception of life provides cultural goods that already carry within them that dissociation of consciousness of which Adorno spoke. That means that cultural formation is a real danger. The cold and violent education of the military dictatorship.

Every culture, far from the effort of the spirit, seems to be leading to this and generations of people are already succeeding each other that have no intention of transforming the world into a place for the fraternal coexistence of all cultures. Education is reduced to a capital.

Capitalist Reductionism

Capitalism itself is a reductionism. Just as patriarchy—its version of gender—is the reduction of the human being to sex (in this case heteronormative binarism between men and women), capitalism is the reduction of life to the economic plan. At the same time, the economy, as well as ecology and all that is structuring the forms of life, are today aspects kidnapped by capitalism, reduced to it.

Capitalism has become the name of a worldview, in which everything becomes inessential relative to the "commodity form" or value-form according to which everything can be bought and sold. In this worldview, thought is undermined by the logic of "income." Living becomes a purely economic issue. The economy becomes a managed way of life with its own rules, such as consumption, personal indebtedness, the security for which one can pay. All this is systemic and, at the same time, somewhat hysterical. Neoliberalism is capitalism in a state of hysteria.

The capital has become the horizon that conducts all the hermeneutics of daily life, to the point of not admitting different ways of thinking and acting in its regime. Capitalism needs to be staged and it costs a lot of money. The act of speaking and even writing, through which we express thoughts, also enters this game which is, after all, a game of language. This is why capitalism is so invested in the order of discourse (what was formerly called rhetoric). The purpose of regulating speech and texts is not to undermine the system. This staging is hysterical, but at the same time it is spectacular, so it works close to art (see the success of cinema in our time) and in the form of a religion. But there is a subtle level of creation of theatricality (hysterical and/or theological) that implies discourse both in real life and in the virtual life of networks.

In this context, words function as stigmata or dogmas that support practice-oriented ideas. If the order of the capitalist discourse is basically theological, it is because it functions as a religion in the field of scriptures and preaching, in general, in the technological pulpit of television which is the most common prosthesis of knowledge among the most economically exploited classes. Just as the word "God" generates, when questioned, the stigma of the heretic or the atheist, the word "capitalist," when questioned, generates the stigma of the "communist," himself treated as a type of atheist in his critical disbelief of the system.

Capitalism depends on the creation of stigmata against everything and all those who come to criticize it: one can use the word "vandal," the term "terrorist," or any other word with an inverted meaning. This is how religion invented the devil as an element of population control. Today, the control of populations through fear serves a real industry of violence and insecurity. In the discursive scheme of the capitalist, stigmatization protects from criticism. Discourse is the capitalism's weapon of protection. Critics, in turn, often avoid saying "capitalism" so they are not accused of being "communists." The logic is this: someone criticizes capitalism and is called a communist for it. The rhetorical games are straightforward and direct, but it is not easy to dismantle them, because there are feelings and interests behind them.

Fascist Rhetoric: Magic Words, Clichés and Distortion

Fascist terminology is composed of clichés. There is a rudimentary epistemology, the effect of the absence of ideas and conceptual work, which has a high impact on the masses and enables the creation of bonds between individuals with poor educational backgrounds or from "semi-formation." The absence of interpretation, the lack of relationship with metaphors and other figures of speech, make the possibility of "talking to a fascist" really limited.

The capitalist seduction that conceals the oppression is organized in the form of a constellation of magical words that serve as clichés, through which the speaker and listener believe they can fulfill all their political desires and obligations. Words such as happiness, ethics, freedom, opportunity, merit, justice, ideology, God, security, but also and negatively others are used in this way: corruption, communism, feminism, gender. Each country will have variations, but in general, they are similar.

Democracy is one of those magic words used by capitalism. Anti-democratic, capitalism needs to hide its only true democracy—the sharing of misery and, today, increasingly, the sharing of death. Fascists will always accuse criticism of being undemocratic, because using words in the form of a mirror is their tactic. Attacking before being attacked, or attacking even if it has already been criticized, is a safe way.

As a covering veil of simple management, democracy used in the magical sense loses its history full of important political meanings. At the same time, it is clear that there is a concrete lie in democracy: the stabilization of capitalism or other authoritarian regimes for which the word serves as a cover. The marriage between oppression and seduction promises to realize capitalist magic in a redemptive fiat lux. Democracy in this context is also reductionism, but we have not yet found a better name for a possible utopia.

Disengagement and dishonesty with what is said have been characteristics of our society for a long time. It is easy for fascism to take advantage of that. The specialized dishonesty of propaganda creates the logic of inversion. Everyone can twist what is said and move on.

We know that we must pay attention to what we are told. On the other hand, it is an ethical duty to pay attention to how we say what we say. Of course, no one will be able to reach a maximum degree of consciousness and always express him or herself in the best way. On the other hand, it is a fact that people often spontaneously manipulate what the other says. Nevertheless, it is not because things are that way that they should not be any different. If the moral level of relationships begins in the "should-be," it is precise because the should-be is not ready and needs to be building. Reversal is a kind of distortion. At the level of relations between private individuals, especially in the private sphere, we can say that the distortion is the fruit of something that we generally call neurosis. It hits every relationship. Parents and children, couples, friends, all those who live together and who, by living together, talk to each other, also distort what each other does and says. To distort in this case is to adapt what actually happened, or what could have happened, to an interpretation useful to some emotional, material or conceptual interest. No speech is made without the consequence of its effects. Knowing this, we constantly hide our interests in what we say.

The logic of inversion depends on the ability to distort. Rhetoric as a field of language defined the strategies of distortion through a classification of fallacies. It may seem quite rational, but in general, it appeals, as any fallacy, to a kind of argumentative dodge. For the inversion is enough to put one thing in the place of the other. Change the place of the speaker, for example. This logic is present both in the victim's guilt and in their victimization.

The inversion, in turn, is not a mere projection, as it may seem. It is a power tactic that goes beyond neurosis and has with it the difference of being a conscious dishonesty. Someone who in the private sphere is a neurotic, in the public sphere can be a scoundrel. The position of the scoundrel is always easy to unravel, but it is not easy to fight. But we live in the empire of gossip where stupidity, both as a cognitive and moral category, has won out. Uncovering it is not worth much anymore. Stupidity has become the whole of power.

The media, in general, including social networks and much of the press, where ideologies and individuals can express themselves freely without limits of ethical and legal responsibility, establish general understandings about facts that come to circulate as truths only because they are repeated. Who knows how to manipulate the vicious and tortuous circle of language wins in terms of power.

The process I have been calling "language consumerism" is the elimination of the political element of language by increasing its demagogic potential. Political emptying is often disguised as a particular expression, a right to free expression. Hysteria, shouting, fallacies and false arguments are very successful, are freely imitated and sound absurd only to those who refuse to buy the logic of distortion in the language market.

The logic of distortion is proper to the consumerism of language. As in all consumerism, language consumerism produces victims, but it also produces the victim's exploiter and the exploiter of the supposed advantage of being a victim. "Advantage" it invents from the logic of the distortion it serves. Victims are there. A reflection on the theme may allow us to think about our postures and impostures when we attack and are attacked at the language level. I think about how people and institutions become victims, sometimes victims, sometimes tormentors of speeches created for the specific purpose of producing violence and destruction. I am not referring to any type of violence that is essential to the discourse as opposed to dialogue, nor to the casual violence of sporadic speech, but to that designed and used as a strategy in gratuitous accusations, defamatory campaigns, swearing in general and also in the creation of a violent context that is capable of fostering a destructive imagination.

We use speeches, but they also use us. Now, we can think about the subjectivity of journalists and television presenters, of politicians and pastors, who speak of lies and defamation and who collaborate in the production of coups d'état, the death of democracies and the advancement of fascism. Those who use speeches can always occupy the position of executioners: they can use their speech against the other, but they can also be used by speeches that they think are authentically their own. What we call discourse, unlike dialogue, always has something ready.

We are built by what we say, and from what we think we are saying. Verbal violence is shared and we are not able to contain it. In fact, would we like to contain it? Is there not among us a deep satisfaction with the easy violence of words that the media know how to manipulate so well? Is there not one who, wanting to fight, enjoys the empty dispute as well as being satisfied with the stupid words of the television agents? Why, after all, do we not count the violence of language in our lives? Large interests are always at stake, but what do small interests of citizens have to do with them?

Inverstion and distortion and distortion do not stop. They also put fascist, macho, racist victimization into action. An example of this type of rhetoric concerns the positioning of those who place themselves in the position of victims of "heterophobia." Some time ago a Member of Congress, known for his homophobia expressed in many ways, appeared as one who "reversed the game" of prejudice putting himself in the position of someone who suffered from "heterophobia." In that view, someone would be the victim of hatred for being a representative of heterosexuality in a society where "homophobia" is the rule. The homophobic tried to produce effects with his gesture: the first would be to reduce the gravity of his usual homophobic gestures, the second would be the trivialization of homophobia, since, it would be something in whose name people act in a banal and, therefore, natural way.

Finally, victims of homophobia would be criminals when they became heterophobic. By changing the place of the victim, by equating the crimes and the victims, we would no longer have victims or criminals, and he, as a criminal, would be unharmed, having succeeded, above all, in making his victim bear the blame of being guilty.

In the same vein, we can cite a deputy, famous for statements that demonstrate serious reflective limitation, who declared himself in public to be a "survivor of an abortion" equating himself to "survivors" of concentration camps, that is, de facto survivors to whom rights are owed, and lowering the experience of those who have experienced actual disasters. Similarly, racist people today speak of racism against whites in a perverse reversal. Whites cannot suffer from racism because racism is a white ideology invented to subdue populations of people marked as black. With racism as an ideology, assassinations and robberies have been guaranteed and the entire history of physical and symbolic violence, which still guarantees structural white privilege, has been justified. What is happening today with the issue of gender also participates in this perverse logic of inversion. In the current agreement between Religion and the State, in which authoritarian priests sell themselves as saints to populations of socially, economically or intellectually weakened people, gender has become a monstrous word.

If gender is an issue that should be part of the Municipal Education Plans in Brazil, religions have begun to speak of "gender ideology."

Armed with bad faith disguised as the protection of strong family values, there are those who are reversing the meaning of the necessary discussion on gender (just as it is necessary to discuss raciality and social class), trying to convince populations that "gender" in itself is not a category for analysis and a field of studies, but a practice of inversion of sexual meaning through which an absurd queer, trans, gay, homosexual dictatorship would be imposed on people. This erases the symbolic liberation of gay and trans life forms against an oppressive heterosexual paradigm in which heterosexuality also functions as a privilege.

"Gender ideology" against which fundamentalists rise up, in the way it is being affirmed, is a fallacious construction. Nevertheless in the current scenario where deception is on the rise, fallacies are very successful. In any of these discourses the marks and suffering of the real victim is diminished. In all these cases, the agents go beyond a misunderstanding or a possible and naive question of self-interpretation. There seems to be more to everyone than just a gap in understanding. We can assume that this gap is, in fact, bad faith, but we can be friendlier and assume that it is only a gap of common sense or reasonableness on the part of those who propose the fallacious argument for abandoning a social and historically critical analysis.

The problem would be formation and education. In practice, they all contribute to the trivialization of the issue of the real victim through their falsehood at the heart of the matter. They all serve to reduce the very serious problem of the rights involved as concrete victims.

Thinking about what may be happening when we see this kind of positioning in the discourse can help us to make the issue of discernment an urgent issue for discussion, which, in addition to easy judgments, is urgent among us.

Ready Thought Victims

In the fascist context, we often do not understand our own thoughts very well, because we are victims of ready-made thoughts.

I say this as simply as I can because I have a deep interest, as a philosophy teacher, in being able to talk to all people in a way that is understood. Understanding is never total, just as the expression of what is meant is never perfect. I know that my way of speaking is extremely limited by my own history, by everything I have studied and by everything I have not studied, felt or lived. This knowledge and this not knowing, when taken seriously, can help us to think better about what we are and what we do.

I believe that the knowledge that is socially important is the one that arises as a result of the dialogue that we have to engage not only with others, but also with ourselves, there, within our consciousness, itself very limited by experience. The knowledge that arises from the encounter of differences is true knowledge. It does not match ready-made ideas with speeches of any kind. It needs dialogue in that sense of the "habitus," of a common space of conviviality. Our knowledge is forged from affective positions, that is, relative to what we feel. And our feelings are easily manipulated. That is exactly what we should not know so that they can continue to be manipulated.

Asking sincerely about what democracy is constitutes an act of cognitive humility, an act that, in my view, inspires democratic practices. Nevertheless it is difficult to do this when we are moved by feelings such as hatred. When resentment commands our way of thinking, we are unable to be aware of the hatred and resentment on which it is based, because hatred is precisely what ends the chance of thought and discernment. The resentment at its root is the discomfort we feel when life is not what we expected it to be.

However if we can ask ourselves this question about what democracy is, we may have a filter to improve our actions. This question, which is conceptual and asks for a definition, can help to break the blockade of our mistreated affections in relation to the collective. At the same time, if I ask myself about my own resentment and hatred, I take an important step toward knowledge. Things are intertwined. Perhaps the question of democracy will lead us to respect the rules of the democratic game, but perhaps it will lead us to wonder what we are doing with each other and with ourselves. Maybe she'll even help us feel better.

Democracy flirts easily with authoritarianism when one does not think about what it is and acts out of impulse or levity, defending, for example, a freedom of expression from violence, or going to the streets to ask for the return of the military dictatorship, as happens from time to time in Brazil. The one who, without thinking, violently imposes his desires or orders; the one who forgets that social life is the life of coexistence and the protection of the rights of all those who live in the same world.

Nobody is democratic if his or her actions do not contribute to the maintenance of democracy as a form of government. Or you forget that everyone needs to be able to respect the rules of the game of democracy. That game involves voting, for example. Voting and election on the basis of the vote must be respected. However this is not what has happened in several countries, especially in Latin America.

That is why, for those who have this understanding of democracy, it is so shocking to see so many people capable of fighting against it. As if they do not benefit from democracy. Those who, in the democratic game, think and act based on double standards, fall into anti-democracy. It is shocking to see people who are fighting against the rights of others and who, because they have not bothered to question what they are doing, are fighting against their own rights without realizing what they are doing. That is the authoritarian citizen. He is practically an anti-citizen.

3

Lynching—Complicity and Murder

When I started to write about facts of everyday life, many things shocked me, but lynching has made the most impression on me. It is a type of violence in which deep social tensions are based, where, although there may be an explanation for it, there is no excuse. Some degree of "excuse," however, is always at the heart of lynching. It is relative to joint action in which everyone acts around an agreement about the truth that governs the motive for lynching. Lynching implies consensus without dialogue. Here, I refer not only to physical lynching, but also to the virtual lynching that is very common on social networks and has a symbolic and practical impact on the lives of many people. There are also those real lynchings provoked by incitement built on social networks such as WhatsApp have an enormous power to spread messages.

The act of lynching configures a hideous type of violence of real people hunting down an individual accused of some kind of illicitness. Many innocent people have been lynched, but even those, who might actually be guilty should be afforded access to the legal sphere so they can receive a fair trial.

Lynchings are shocking by their disproportionate levels of violence. This is a crime committed by a group against a helpless individual. As is the procedure of "all against one." Secondly, because escape from lynching is only possible by a miracle. In the midst of the collective, no one dares to defend the victim. Nobody is going against the mob. The action does not admit doubt or reflection, therefore, it can stay quiet.

What makes someone participate in the act like a lynch mob? Three elements combine to allow action: the first and most fundamental is the annulment of subjectivity—whoever participates in a lynching is not capable of thinking about what they do; second, the absence of compassion, the human capacity to put themself in somebody else's shoes, to imagine somebody else's pain; and, finally, a desire to be part of the mob. A strange "take place" can call anyone to destroy someone "along with" others. We have experienced this in television audiences of reality shows where the potential exterminator is at stake.

What kind of "community" could lynch someone? What someone is doing in the act of lynching is, for themselves, more than right. Someone relies on the others' gesture. There is a deep cowardice in the act of lynching that no one can miss. The idea that the mob, as well as each individual presents sufficient proof that their act is justified. Asking whether an idea and gesture might be different is impossible for the eventual owner of the reason. There is no distrust in the process, there's only truth. The consequence is that everyone feels allowed to kill. However one never does it alone, always with the help of someone else. So those involved do not have to feel responsible for their act. Subjective profit is the result of perversion of the moral order: the guarantee of irresponsibility.

The spontaneous mob are made up of individuals full of hatred who find their place in the collective. The place where each one can let loose the paranoid impulse that can exist within them. The community that kills rises above complicity in cowardice. The hypothesis of the collective cruel agent is that the "lynched" is some kind of heinous criminal. How can those who commit the crime of lynching feel morally superior if they commit a heinous crime?

In the logic of murder, the other has to die. Why does the lynch mob think they can punish another with their bare hands? The lynch mob practices, against the victim, the guilt of which they themselves are the bearer. Guilt they are trying to get rid of in the act of beating someone else to death. The lynch-monger purges their own hatred projecting it onto a helpless stranger. The criminal is the other, so the other is immediately punished. The process is a reversal.

We already know the banality of life and death in our culture. What authorizes someone or a mob to kill? It is the same logic as the generalized corruption. There is a mental and ideological rule that governs our life in common: "If the other does, I can do it too." But how is this reasoning created? In my opinion, there is a logic of endorsement. In the hordes of militias that terrify minorities in real and virtual life, everyone is a potential victim; everyone can be the hunt of the day.

Without thought, killing is an increasingly easy act. It depends on the increasingly widespread irresponsibility and cowardice that imputes itself to the other, freeing oneself from responsibility for one's actions.

The Banality of Death

Fascist times are cold and harsh. Times when there are many variations of death—death by neglect and murder, death by abandonment, death by suicide—and little or no reflection on death. Thinking about death takes its toll on the era of banal happiness typical of those times when all anguish is avoided, when social networks only want to know about photos featuring smiling people and wonderful scenes. The fascist feels no anguish because death is not an option for him. He does not remember he is going to die. He does not die symbolically, as happens to people in general sometimes in life. Now, the fascist does not die because he cannot die. He does not die precisely because, as his rigidity confirms, he is already somehow dead.

Before being a medical or biological category, life is a political category. As a political category, life implies our power for the symbolic relationship with the other, which is always a relationship of recognition. Outside of that, there is death.

The corpse is the total objectification. And there are subjective corpses. Dead souls with no chance of establishing a relationship with the other. There are those dressed as the dead who pretend to be alive among us. In suits and ties, they deliver the political rules of the game to the others who remain alive. The corpse wears the fantasy of the professional politician and rises to the spectacular stage of the media. There he launches his rotten vomit against the dance of life that is the Dionysian dance of difference.

On the political scene, some people think it would be better to die for good. Some people become depressed and think about killing themselves. In countries like Brazil, depression has become a political category.

Today it is not enough to avoid talking about suicide. Indeed, the reinvention of life is necessarily political. The question we can ask ourselves is whether a fascist would be capable of meditating on his own death at the present political moment.

It is grief, which in many ways is avoided; at the same time that depression advances. Understanding the state of grief in our culture can help us understand what has been done in terms of the social and cultural management of the suffering we experience today. If we remember Freud's definition of mourning,[1] it would be the loss of an object that would imply a psychic work to get used to life after it. Grief would be normal when overcome.

So far, there is nothing out of the ordinary. People's lives would be organized with the organization of pain. Suffering and pain would once again be part of everyday life. The grief, the overcoming work. Everyone will, at some point, live the feeling of grief because it is impossible to live a lifetime without becoming attached to other people. Living would mean loss and mourning, for those who experienced it.

One thinks, then, of the conditions of the "I," of the subjective personal fragility of those who are experiencing "depression". From this point of view, everything is thrown onto the "subjectivity" of the individual as if it were "natural" and not socially constructed. This position is not sustained when we see the social, collective and cultural

---

[1] Freud, Sigmund. "Trauer und Melancholie." In: *Werke aus den Jahren 1913-1917*. Frankfurt am Main: Fischer, 2010.

conditions in which mourning takes place today. In this sense, in a time when the cultural industry of libido and happiness is on the rise encouraging everyone to believe that nothing is lost and that everything can be conquered, that there is no suffering in the world of consumption, grief is not very welcome. In a way, grief is a counter-ideological state. Grief damages social functioning because it represents a state of opposition to life. Grief interrupts production and consumption. Therefore, it is socially demanded that grief happens quickly.

In order for the system machine to continue working, we need to be deprived of grief every day, forbidden to live the experience of loss, forbidden to lose. The ban on mourning is related to the trivialization of death. And the trivialization of death is related to the trivialization of life. Summoned to a bizarre idea of progress, we are forbidden to suffer and to fail. What the depressed live through is, in fact, a kind of warning against bereavement, as if they had no right to their own suffering. If someone do not have the right to his or her own biography and body, why to have the right to own suffering?

The life of a bereaved person could be depressing. However, life is even sadder when one cannot elaborate mourning in societies that avoid it, as the capitalist society is. Carrying out the work of mourning in the context of an ideology of production and consumption lived as the only dimensions of life becomes, today, an act of spiritual heroism. This is how "depressed" is the stigma of those who cannot return to the norm of success, of plastic happiness in the scope of action emptied in the productive-consumer scheme that governs the daily life of people submitted to the spirit of capitalism.

In this context, one might wonder if the depressed and their depression do not have something to teach us about the general state of society.

Nietzsche wrote about his famous theory of eternal return in a paragraph of *The Gay Science* titled "The Heaviest Weight."[2] In the case of this doctrine, it is a question of the weight of repression, of what cannot be forgotten. The affection that, dense and painful, is somehow taken away by life. Each human individual has some pain, or several pains that are, in the sense of what psychoanalysis calls trauma, constitutive of his subjective condition. How one experiences what one might call a personal wound—such as the wound that Ivan Ilitch in Tolstoy's tale experiences in silence and solitude—depends on many factors. It is true that suffering cannot be measured, but when narrated by someone who suffers, we realize that it takes on different intensities.

As in Nietzsche's text, the intensity of suffering is constantly expressed by its "weight." Therefore, the question involved in the doctrine of the eternal Nietzschean return, concerns the reason for carrying weight. In other words, the question of Nietzsche is at stake as to why suffering cannot be overcome, why there is certain suffering that seems to weigh more. What, then, do we do with what weighs on us, since no one should voluntarily wish to carry a burden? Precisely because of this, because it is difficult to carry the weight, one tends to throw it somewhere. We can say that, in the effort to get rid of it, we tend to throw it in the direction of the other.

---

2 Nietzsche, Friedrich. *Die Fröliche Wissenchaft*. München: Carl Hanser, 1994.

At the same time, it is not because things weigh on us that we need to carry them, but because we carry them that they weigh on us. Now what weighs is that which cannot be released, that which cannot be left behind. This is best understood when Nietzsche, in *Thus Spoke Zarathustra*,[3] uses a dead man as a metaphor for the weight one carries. Resentment, in this case, can be the uninterrupted feeling of pain that one day was felt, like the dead man that Zarathustra has on his back. He would disappear if we had the capacity to forget what was negatively felt and, from then on, learn to accept what happened to us. That would be what Nietzsche called "Amor Fati" the "love of fate". It is the love to what someone is, to what happens to someone. To forget, in the face of resentment, would be a kind of virtue proper to those who live the love of fate. It would be, in the case of confrontation with what has been lived in terms of weight, an act of encouragement to the lightness that could be achieved with love. Lightness, contrary to weight, would be a force in this case.

To love destiny would be, first of all, an act of detachment. It would be the act of accepting the weight of things, not their abstract denial. This acceptance would allow us to leave things in the middle of the way, abandon them to ourselves and, through this abandonment (totally dialectical), return them to themselves. To history, to time, to space. In this case, we would experience suffering, pain, the affections of love—and also hatred—but at the moment when they would present themselves as part of life and not as dead weight.

---

[3] Nietzsche, Friedrich. *Also sprach Zarathustra/Thus Spoke Zarathustra*: German/English Bilingual Text. JiaHu Books, 2013.

This means that the doctrine of "amor fati" would be the doctrine of acceptance of affections. When it would be evident that not feeling is impossible, but feeling again can be better elaborated in the direction of a future affection. For an open affection forward to the future. Love can be defined as being an affection open to the future. Hate can be defined as being an affection closed for the future.

The "love of destiny" would imply abandoning the dead weight of resentment in the middle of the road. It would therefore be an act that would relativize the weight. To leave the weight of the past to the past would be like giving it back, generously, thus renewing the place of the future.

Nietzsche used weight as a negative metaphor applied to affectivity. However as dialectical glasses improve our vision, we should see what weight and lightness are measures of value. In the same way that we can say "heavy weight" or "light weight" for the strength of a professional fighter, weight is always a measure that implies the "greater" or "lesser." It implies a higher or lower value and a weight—or a price—to be paid when it comes to some balance.

In a society in which misery and wealth are confused in the market and in the church, the power of the wretched is in accumulated suffering. The power of the oppressor is in producing that weight. It is the same thing that doesn't allow you to change the course of history. We know that the most resentful is the owner of the greatest suffering, a suffering that someone thinks is greater than that of others when seen from his own point of view. It is the resentment expressed in the victim's speech. It is also, and much more, resentment that blames the other for being a victim. The issue is the resentment of those who are unable to see the feelings of others; at least, to suspect something about their suffering.

Even greater is the resentment that manages the resentment of others. That is the resentment of the owner of the means of production of resentment. The media, churches, businesses, states, political and economic regimes generate this resentment by creating the eternal return of suffering.

Resentment hides hatred and is the origin of fascism that "weighs" on our current culture. In the gesture of every fascist—be it the homophobic, the macho, the racist, the one who defends class inequality, or the superior "nature" of some against others, in the subtle fascism of the capitalist who says that things cannot be different—is resentment, synonymous with hatred, a mark of the impossibility of going beyond oneself, of producing a better world for all. In that resentment is our inability to deal with death, our need to repress it and, in its eternal return, to live the destructive potential of the death drive as if it were life. Today we can say that hatred is the heaviest of all weights. Hatred is the basis of fascism. Resentment is its complex name. Its opposite implies the loving and wasteful feast of freedom in the opposite direction of the spirit of death, which is the avaricious spirit of the economic system.

The fact that hatred is attracting attention among us, generating the anti-political scenario that we know, is a sign that we can overcome it. It is a sign that love still exists as a widely political affection, as a power against resentment, against the hatred that is refined every day, with its miasma always ready to suffocate anyone who is alive.

The Culture of Harassment

In the macho culture of disrespect and violence, "moral harassment" and "sexual harassment" have been the rule for a long time. This macho and disrespectful culture is anti-dialogical and, necessarily, fertile soil for fascism. Such types of harassment would not develop so easily if they did not find a socially conducive climate. Harassment is another of those cultural patterns that, to varying degrees and intensities, reaches all spheres of life. We can therefore speak of a culture of "harassment," that is to say, a culture in the "spirit" of harassment in which human relations develop, in which the "moral" and "sexual" questions are written.

Harassment is an unethical practice of oppression based on direct pressure on an individual. The stalker pushes the individual he is stalking stalker to do his will.

That the harasser is not capable of seeing in the other a subject, first of all seeing in him an object, does not take away the responsibility for any of his actions, but explains the context in which, in some way, the great majority does not ask themselves the question of the other. The harassment society forms people capable of undertaking harassment and to consent to it. It is as if there was an authorization established in the social sphere—that each one introjects, when treating the other as a thing—so that the other is not valued as a subject of rights. The harasser acts with the endorsement of the lack of recognition—of respect and even empathy toward the other—as a widespread practice at the cultural level.

Institutions demand performance from their indebted and defaulted individuals. The State collects taxes and obedience to laws, the Family collects actions related to gender roles and financial responsibilities, the School collects success and obedience, the world of Work collects production, the Economy in its current state collects consumption. The harassment society is a network organized around the performance with a view to the maintenance of these institutions in which individuals have the chance to self-conserve only if they are able to meet the standard required to maintain the institution.

The one who does not correspond is missing. The lack is relative to not performing something properly. That is where the blame lies. Nietzsche, at the end of the nineteenth century, identified as a feeling of guilt this lack planted in someone by the pressure to correspond to a set of oppressive moral rules. No matter what the time or the content of this morality, the fact is that there is always a morality, always a standard to follow, and the guilt corresponding to the powerlessness to adapt to it. The evil in this case is feeling inadequate. The inadequate will do anything to eliminate the guilt without knowing that it cannot be expiated within the framework of a society whose principle of performance is at stake.

That is how the harassment society is the blame society. Indebtedness, which has become so common at the compulsive level in today's capitalism, is the gesture that seeks to contain guilt. The culprit is the victim who does not know he is a victim. The harassment society is the one that needs to create mechanisms to collect what it wants as a result.

It is in this context that propaganda becomes the institution responsible for the daily harassment of individuals to want and buy.

Advertising does not act on simple seduction. Seduction would not be so insistent. Seduction is for Don Juan as is rape for advertising. The insistence aims at the consent of the victim.

Advertising is a case of violence that needs the approval of the victim; it needs the adherence, so it is not exactly—or only—a case of rape. It is precisely harassment, a type of violence that hides its violence.

Basically, layers and layers of cultural agreements to which the victim must adhere cover violence. Harassment is the violence that is hidden in the appearance of seduction. The inherent expectation of the culture of harassment is that rape will not be necessary because the victim will surrender easily.

"Relax and enjoy" is the cynical sentence that endorses the link between harasser and harassed, giving victory to the harasser. There is no desire in this "jouissance." The administration of desire is, in fact, the victim's guilt. It is necessary to make it seem as if the harassed person wants it. He must believe that he has some advantage. Without believing in this advantage, he could rebel and lose everything. It is supposed to be a docile victim. Hence the practice must seem somewhat impotent. The pedophilic character of all harassment, so to speak, has to do with this appearance of weakness in the act itself, which is addressed to someone who is not responsible and who must, in some way, consent to what is done with him. Propaganda aimed at children is, one of the most cruel examples here, because childhood is the stage of life where the basic structures of subjectivity are created—the structures that will permit discernment, judgment, and reflection relative to all spheres of life.

The child trusts the adult, just as the citizen, downgraded to the consumer, trusts advertising.

The harassed man is a victim, but above all, he's a subject of law. This fact must be sought to be hidden, so that the culture of harassment reproduces itself infinitely.

The Logic of Rape

Hate sustains the culture of violence. One of the best-known is hatred against women, which is called misogyny.[4] Misogyny is a naturalized hatred that involves from symbolic violence entrenched in the history of literature, to radical violence such as feminicide and mass extermination of women as we see in the passage from the Middle Ages to Modena in the episode known as Witch Hunt.

A book by historian Georges Duby[5] contains a story that helps us to understand a culture of disrespect that, at its extreme, passes through machismo and reaches fascism, even before that term existed. According to Duby, a certain Gervais of Tilbury, walking among the vineyards in the Champagne region, happened upon a girl. In the account, Gervais of Tilbury finds her attractive, speaks to her "courteously of lewd love," and prepares to go further. She treats him rudely, refuses, "If I lose my virginity, I'll be condemned." Without understanding how she could resist him, he concludes that she is a

---

[4] Bloch, R. Howard. *Medieval Misogyny and the Invention of Western Romantic Love.* Chicago: University of Chicago Press, 1992.

[5] Duby, Georges. *Dames du XIIe Siécle.* Paris: Gallimard, 1995.

heretic who considers any copulation as diabolical. He tries to convince the girl, but he cannot. He denounces her, she is arrested, tried and burned as a witch. And that is because his argument against her is indisputable evidence.

Considering the Church's stance against sex outside marriage at that time, the narrative shows the perversion of the posture of her murderer: the girl was trapped, she either gave in or she died. Giving in or resisting, she had no way out. The proof of his condemnation was "incontestable"—after all, it was proof presented by a cleric, a man of the Church! It would be infinitely perverse if it were not, at the same time, frighteningly current.

This situation reveals what we can call the "logic of rape," as it still works today in our way of thinking about the relationships between men and women (I am talking about men and women in view of the fact that these categories are what put this type of violence into play.) In the logic of rape, the victim—a woman—has no way out: in any case she will be condemned when, beforehand and without analysis, she has already been convicted whether or not she gives in to rape. The victim is always questioned according to the logic of rape, which, since the time of the Inquisition, has been as an object with which the subject could do whatever he wanted. The criminal is not questioned, because he is a man, and according to the logic of rape, a man is not objectified, a man is not blamed, for his violence. Women are always to blame as every individual proscribed who awakens the desire for proscription. In other words, the victim arouses the desire to attack.

In the logic of rape, any and all blame lies with the victim, so the rapist is not held responsible for his act. A rapist cannot do that alone.

He needs the support of a lot of people, a whole society. In the Middle Ages, a clergyman would have the full support of the Church and the court that functioned according to its laws made by priests: the court of the "Holy" Inquisition. "Holy," in this case, is not a simple irony but a perversion.

Now, as yesterday, no rapist who wants to take responsibility for his act. This is where society can help. The act of taking responsibility implies the ability to recognize that other persons' injured by an act have the right to claim compensation and the right to demand protection against a crime. The rapist is not to blame because he acts within the socially sustained logic, which implies a "reason" for things. Either the rapist acts as did the rapist of the medieval tale who acted because of his "nature"— his "reason"—granting himself "the right" to have sex with a woman he meets, regardless of whether that woman wants to have sex with him.

This is absurd if we think along democratic lines, but it is not absurd if we think along the lines of rape, which is undemocratic and authoritarian in its most intimate sense, and which serves to absolve those in power of responsibility. Machismo and fascism have in common the production of a victim who is treated as guilty.

In the case of the story told earlier, the woman was not raped by Gervais, but was considered by him to be "rapeable." She was burned at the stake because she refused to have sex. However, Gervais did not see the rape and violence of her act. At stake, according to his rape logic, was his "right." The sex involved was not considered heinous or diabolical—but the woman who refused to obey him was considered a witch who was to be punished by fire.

Using a projective mechanism by which she should give in to an "irresistible" man, rape itself was, in that context, only a kind of "logical" sex in the authoritarian head of the rapist. Gervais did not consider that he had committed a crime. Furthermore, why wasn't that a crime? Because he and his institution (the Church) had made up the rules. He and his institution perverted the meaning of things and accused the other of not having understood that meaning. The young woman who was the victim, in this case, is the one who was accused of a crime in a perverse inversion that only the logic of rape is capable of sustaining because she is the elementary logic of universal machismo to which women have been submitted for a long time.

By the logic of rape, a woman is always "hunted," "caught." By the logic of rape, one thinks more of the victim's "mistake" than the criminal's "mistake." It is as if the victim was guilty of not having escaped, of not having run faster, of not having disappeared beforehand. In Brazil and in many other countries, such as India—to give an example of a country with one of the highest global incidences of rape—the logic of rape means that women need to camouflage themselves in order to survive. Unfortunately still, well protected, they'll be raped. Even with the most protective clothes, because, like the girl desired by Gervais, the rapist will think like Gervais.

Better not to look "like a woman", the logic of rape prays. It should be added, that in the logic of rape, at the same time, women are objectified by the cultural industry of pornography, in advertising, in cinema, in fashion, in magazines and television programs of the so-called "feminine universe," one of the most successful traps in the invention of the "feminine ideal." In the logic of rape, ambiguity reigns: being a woman has two weights and two measures that are always dictated according to the logic of rape typical of masculinist, macho society, in short, the patriarchal logic.

The logic of rape defines the victim as being guilty. Now, the logic of rape is not other than that of domination in general, but applied to women. It is the same logic that allowed white "owners" of blacks enslaved by them—to deprive them of their freedom, and to beat and kill people of color. It is the same logic, unfortunately, that applies on the part of the government—or the owners of power in general—to the poor today.

Considering also that the ample campaign "I don't deserve to be raped," that circulated through the Internet in countries like Brazil, had reactive effects such as manifestations organized by groups of men that, as heirs of Gervais, the medieval rapist, affirm "I have the right to be macho," we can meditate a little more on the rape mentality, unfortunately common both in men and women. It is worrying that many men and women, claim or accept the idea that "women who wear clothes that show the body deserve to be attacked."

People in general cannot be said to be in favor of violence against women purely and simply, but they understand that rape is a "different" type of violence because of something that women have done—hence the question of "deserving." This violence that is rape—in the logic of rape—is a violence that is somehow "deserved" by the victim who, strictly speaking, is no longer considered a victim, but, in a perverse inversion, becomes the "guilty" party. Rape is the act in which the other—the victim—has no chance of defense because *a priori* they have already been condemned.

In the logic of rape that governs society, the verdict that is thrown at any woman is: "You are condemned to rape." And why is that? Because, according to this logic, the woman is ontologically condemned for being/appearing to be like a woman. In her appearance, her aesthetic condition, only reveal her ontological condition, then the rapist's attention turns to her clothes. Because clothes accentuate the female form making women, in someway "predisposed to rape, fit for rape."

It is important to realize that the logic of rape is the same logic that the Nazi regime applied to Jews in the 1940s in Germany; that the Israeli State applies to Palestinians today; that the French applied to Nigerians; that the owners of large food stores such as McDonald's apply to their customers and employees; that the governments of several countries apply to the poor under the current military police regime; that the Brazilian agro-business manager applies to Brazilian Amerindians. They are only a few examples from around the world. Hate for the other is stated in many ways, many are victims of patriarchal hatred—capitalist, Judeo–Christian–Islamic, European— and women have always been special victims of this hatred directly directed at them in the home and in all the visual or virtual spaces in which they have been transformed into objects mystified by misogynistic ambiguity that, at times, they praise in order to better dominate.

Men themselves, potential rapists, may wonder about the meaning of being something like a "man" in our world, in view of the possibility of rape. It is up to the whole of society to think about the victim, but also the little perceived figure of the "rapist subject" who, except for a few exceptions, is always a "man"—any exception that may be raised will confirm the general rule that rape is carried out by men against women and against all those who have characteristics considered feminine, homosexual and transvestite. Children and animals included.

I would like to raise some important aspects to be considered, in an attempt to think of the male condition as potentially rapist. The central question I have in mind is, "How does one become a rapist?" I think this question may help us to think about the rapist that society—parents, teachers, institutions, mass media—creates every day. The rapist is the one who sees himself having a strange "right to rape," as the one who claims the "right to be a sexist." He can only think like that because he is an authoritarian personality who, as such, does not have the capacity to see the "other." Paranoid, he feels like the center of the world, the world in which he is the king and the woman is, at best, a servant. In this sense, every rapist is like Gervais of Tilbury, he finds himself an irresistible. And, like the medieval canon, he thinks he is absolutely right when he desires a woman and decides to burn her at the stake because he did not get from her what he wanted. Like Gervais de Tilbury, the rapist, who claims from the "Holy" Inquisition of society the right to be macho and to demean and violate women, is also a "hysterical" who moves a world—social networks, for example—to hide the narcissistic wound that rejection has produced in him. He disguises himself until he annihilates the other so he can be something. Many have never thought about the serious question of male hysteria because, in the logic of rape, one should only think that women are hysterical.

Thus the rapist, authoritarian and irresponsible, but above all hysterical himself, claims the male supremacy in which he is pleased.

We still live in the Middle Ages. Only by reversing the logic of rape will we escape it.

Myth and Resentment—Brazil Repressed

The power of myth is the explanation of the unknown. Myth can be the traditional narrative of a people—whether native to India, Greece or the Americas—translating their ancestral truth, but it can also be the fabrication of "truth," "essence," and "nature," in order to sustain ideological interests. There is, therefore, a difference between myth as a narrative of origin and myth as an illusory social construction. In the latter case, the myth shows something to hide another. It is in this sense that I will use it here to talk about the "national myth" of Brazil.

Like the image of a country—which is built—it is an issue that involves internal and external aspects of this country. We can say, through this image, that Italy is this, Ireland is that, Japan is that, or that Angola is like that. We rarely stop to think that there is some interest behind the definitions: the interest in "framing," in transforming the unknown into something known as identification. It is no exaggeration to think that behind the act of defining is the attempt to dominate what is strange thus, transforming it into something familiar, eliminating or controlling its strangeness. If we remember the gesture of Christopher Columbus— who did not learn the language of the people he met—arriving in the Americas and defining the people he met as "Indians" because he believed he had arrived in the Indies, we have a good example of the danger of "identifying" and, in the sequence, of defining the stranger, the "other"—as if this other fits within a known and proper category. We continue to look with Columbus' eyes, when we identify the unknown with the known, the complex with the simple, the other with the same. We live in the deepest "Columbus complex"[6] incapable of recognizing what is different.

Faced with these explanations by identification, which configure the myth of the Brazilian, we are obliged to ask ourselves: "What is it to be Brazilian?" taking into account that this question is highly problematic, considering that we live in the era of singularity. We need to ask ourselves if there is sense in defining a particular "Brazilian," or the "Brazilian people" who being the result of an interweaving of diverse historical, social and political processes, are one of the most difficult peoples to define in today's world? The Brazilian people are so heterogeneous, culturally speaking, that they do not curve to identity.

Besides, wouldn't trying to define Brazilians—their "Brazilian-ness"—continue the act of reproducing their "myth," as a forced explanation.

Legally, a Brazilian is someone who was born in Brazil or became naturalized by living here, incorporating its cultural aspects. Defining the Brazilian culture is somewhat complicated, because Brazil is not a uniform country in the sense of its daily habits and artistic, urban, rural, and musical expressions, nor even its varied climate and geography. If we look for the "natural" Brazil, we will find the "cultural"

---

[6] Tiburi, Marcia. *Complexo de Vita-Lata: análise da humilhação brasileira (Mongrel complex: analysis of the Brazilian humiliation)*. Rio de Janeiro: Record, 2021.,

Brazil, and if we find the "cultural" Brazil, it is not simple either. It is true that our political history—which involves colonization, slavery and a great dictatorship from which we freed ourselves less than 30 years ago, in addition to a democracy in an embryonic state— guarantees us a common resentment. The Portuguese language— imposed on various immigrant groups less than 100 years ago during the Vargas dictatorship— unites in the same resentful way a country which produces illiterate people due to neglect and state abandonment. The language of colonization that we are invited to love does not contemplate the languages of immigrants, or of native peoples, or African peoples who arrived here not as immigrants, but in the position of slaved people.

A Brazilian who travels to another country will not be surprised if the inhabitants of the country visited see in Brazil only the image of carnival, samba and beautiful women always available for some kind of easy sex. The image of Brazil outside Brazil includes the Amazon, Rio de Janeiro and samba. Brazil is associated with the jungle and its dangers, its coastline and other natural and tourist riches. The image of Brazil outside Brazil is that of football, of a hospitable and peaceful and simple people, of rascality, and, necessarily, of self-confident poverty.

The colonial condition both inside and outside Brazil, is erased with such naturalness. Brazil would be a country where people are happy, according to the strange ideal of happiness sold on postcards. In this imaginary country, it is believed that people are "in a good mood," they do not complain because, despite a corrupt policy and terrible social conditions, always taken advantage of by a certain cultural industry of violence, people would not have the temperament to demand changes or to act in a different direction with their own hands.

In the imagination of non-Brazilians and even of Brazilians, Brazil has long been transformed into what it is not. The recalculated Brazil is not remembered in any image that is built on Brazil. They forget the drought and the growing deforestation that is transforming the forest into a desert. Those who see the beaches forget the vast lands taken by colonization between the states. It does not see the country that long ago erased the image of its decimated indigenous people who are still being murdered in conflicts with large landowners in the name of agribusiness. The country that also hides the murder of women, homosexuals, transvestites and the poor, that hides drug trafficking, that hides corrupt politicians financed by unidentified companies. A country that hides the general ignorance fostered every day by the absence of a real education project for the people. A country seized by fascism.

Brazil is not carnival and extreme violence is hidden, but it comes to the fore when it comes to using fear as a stimulus for security to be sold. Brazilians living in Brazil accept to a great extent the other's view of himself, whether the foreigner, the cultured intellectual, or the means of communication that feed social imaginary. And since the conditions—educational and cultural—required to show other visions of Brazil are not available, this helps to feed the vision of a stereotyped Brazil. In order to change this view, it would be necessary to analyze what is repressed in the culture itself, which would imply reviewing the symbolic scenario, but also the impressive social inequality of our country covered by a fundamental aspect of the Brazilian myth that is its rapid development in recent years until the death of its democracy in 2016.

If the society of the spectacle lives from the production of stereotypes, Brazil and the countries of Latin America is a relatively easy commodity. In all stereotypes, the stereotype of "natural" Brazil weighs. The cultural industry of tourism has allied itself to the myth of the country of sex as something also natural. The idea of a country of prostitution should not appear even when we know that many foreigners come to Brazil to exercise sex tourism, which is fought internally by certain people and institutions. The child prostitution that serves foreigners is hidden because it damages Brazil's own marketable image. The hypocritical agreement is always previously signed by the silence that guarantees the progress of injustices and violence in the maintenance of the general national narrative. Today, we can say that unusual aspect of our culture comes to the surface disturbing previous understandings. For example, the publication in 1936 of Sérgio Buarque de Holanda's book *Roots of Brazil*,[7] which challenged the idea of Brazilian "cordiality" and had a major impact both on the scientific interpretation and common sense in general.

This cliché, taken as truth, is not usually questioned. Certain lower- and even middle-social classes have a high work and study load. In Brazil there is an immense population of workers who study in precarious universities hoping that, through disproportionate efforts, they can overcome their social and economic conditions in the face of all sorts of adversities. The manifestations of recent times show that cordiality, accommodation and political disinterest no longer portray the lives of the people who live in Brazil, if they ever did.

---

[7] Holanda. Sérgio Buarque de. *Raízes do Brasil*. Rio de Janeiro: José Olympio, 1971.

The Eurocentric Paradigm

The Eurocentric paradigm characterized by the precarious principle of identity regarding the vision of the "other" is part of the history of the Americas and Brazil. Represented in the texts of Columbus, Cortez and other "conquerors," the Eurocentric paradigm continues based on certain negative discourses the Amerindian peoples. I am thinking here of feedback between journalist and the public, as Gabriel Tarde explained.[8] We are in the whirlwind of hatred between reality and discourse that must be evaluated in order to forge a more just society to which theory—as an essential practice of reflection—can contribute.

In the process of cover-up to which they give rise, such discourses in which the question of "subalternity" is always constructed by the cynical nexus between knowledge and power, maintain the unethical foundation of a historical genocide against the Amerindian peoples. Only this genocide will sustain the maintenance of native peoples' land takeover. This European invasion of "Amefrican" life as Lélia Gonzales said.[9] In order to sustain itself, it needs public and political support that will make it stand as a truth, socially valid and unquestioned, thus guaranteeing its success. The way in which Amerindian peoples are treated in this matter of land grabs, a fascist way that includes government and civil society, clashes with the democratic desire of much of the population today.

---

[8] Tarde, Gabriel. *La opinion et la foule*. CreateSpace Independent Publishing Platform, 2016.

[9] Gonzales, Lélia; Haselbalg, Carlos. *Lugar de negro*. Rio de Janeiro: Marco Zero, 1982.

The discourse of the colonizing alliance not only denies a place for the "other" by projecting on it a truth that does not concern it, but, it also, only achieves this effect if, rather, it substantializes this other as "negative." According to the logic of the principle of identity, negativity is what, in the order of culture, emerges as something undesirable.

What I want to say is that ethical and political consequences arise in the process of making "negative" by the word, by the text. The discourse sustains in its false background, in the last instance, the foundation of the Amerindian genocide, since it is constituted as the violent base from which violence itself is hidden. We can call this process hermeneutic violence. I am referring to the death of the other that can only happen under his cover, never in the open, never in a direct and legally authorized death penalty, but much earlier in a dismissal of the other from his affirmation as something negative. Genocide, in principle somewhat frightening, has become a true cultural practice, concealed in anti-indigenous discourses in general, with the endorsement of the media in accordance with common sense and the negligence of society as a whole in relation to the indigenous question.

Genocide is, therefore, the very name of the ideology that governs the relationship between the "Brazilians" and the indigenous question, as well as the Europeans and the colonial question, against which a few take on the challenge of acting against silence. It is not wrong to say that we live in the age of genocide. We can even say that, as a Brazilian nation, we were born from genocide while the murder of others is part of our collective history. "Massacrifice" was a term used by Todorov,[10]

---

[10] Todorov, Tzvetan. *The conquest of America the question of the other*. Translated from the french by Richard Howard. London, Harper Colophon Books, 1984.

which brought together sacrifice and massacre to explain what happens in a society in which killing is culturally justified in everyday life and, at the same time, hidden and denied.

Hermeneutic Violence—The Question of the Other

What we can call "otherness" is a hermeneutic question. To say who the "other" is, I need to express something about it. The problem is that the "other" is always someone or something I do not know on principle. It is the "principle of identity" that leads us to think from assumptions that reduce what is different from what we know. Overcoming this mentality is not an effort that depends only on one individual or another, but on historical processes of which we are part. There are intellectual processes for which we need to take responsibility as builders of theories, as educators and, indeed, as the simple individuals that we are. Now, what can be said of the "other" is always only an interpretation, in the sense that something is placed before a point of view. The distance between the thing and the point of view is usually forgotten or disregarded by the "point of view" which is only a point of view by assuming its own position in a system where the "truth" is disputed. What is said about the "other" is always said by someone who supposes it, whom we can call by the term "same."

The "same" suffers from the limits of the horizon of understanding in which it is established and, when it is established, it establishes the "other." The same is precisely the one that appears at the limit of an understanding that is relative to another in relation to which the "same" is not disposed of as "relative." What it says about the other can easily derive from ready-made and precarious discourses when they are motivated by sociocultural aspects, such as morality and religion, class understanding, and even hidden, unconscious desires and interests.

Tristan Todorov in *The Conquest of America*, examines the question of the other in an analysis of conquerors like Columbus and Cortez who, reaching the world of the Americas, a world unknown to them, interpreted it according to the inevitable limits to their own perspective. Such limits are, curiously, those of the knowledge that they are representatives and are effective in the way communication is established with the found other. Communication is part of the desire to know, but it also implies a morality: wanting to relate to the other is what is at stake.

At stake is the fact that we take what we have already seen, that we suppose to know, as true and absolute knowledge, when it is the belief that allows us to interpret the "other" that manifests itself. This knowledge/belief, at the same time that it leads to an interpretation, in a certain way clogs up the encounter with the novelty that would be inherent in some knowledge—as true as possible—of the unknown other. If interpretation seems unavoidable, it must be taken into account that its limits are inevitable. The relationship between it and the other has been worked on throughout the history of European philosophy since pre-Socratic philosophers. In all the tradition that derives from Plato, the other (heteron) is a principle of being. In modern European philosophy, the relationship between the same and the other has been translated into terms of subject and object. Of a thinking being and a thinking thing.

The question we must ask ourselves is whether it would be possible to think and act beyond the relationship between subject and object? In *On Subject and Object,* Theodor Adorno comments that "the subject devours the object, by forgetting how much itself is object."[11] In other words, what the "subject" forgets is the mediation that exists between him and what is called an object. In this case, a game of weakness and strength is in force, dialectic between the objective and subjective forces that sustain this subject–object system while they are guaranteed by it. What we call subject also suffers from the objectivity of the discourse of other "subjects" who do not perceive how much they themselves are objects. Adorno spoke of "primacy of the object" to designate the fact that the subject becomes an object, the fact that the object says something against the subject's intentionality, against his "prior knowledge" of the object. In simple terms: the object is that which resists what the subject wants to make of it, but, at the same time, the object is unfortunately that which the subject makes of his other.

We can think about all this from the point of view of the strategy of reduction to the body, analogous to the construction of a heteroconstructed identity. Both are part of the strategy of practical fallacy that unites discourse and action in the process of "framing" which is also a process of "marking" the other so that he or she stays in a controllable place. Such is the place of identity. The individual invaded by Columbus was "marked" by his worldview, objectified as long as it was placed within an identity by frame. Within which their bodies were objectified. Someone wondered if they had souls, a factor

---

[11] Adorno, Theodor. *Stichworte: Kritische Modelle II*. Suhrkamp, 1969.

that could somehow "bring them closer" to the condition of the European man.

This estrangement from difference defines that whoever called "Indian" was identified in a difference in relation to the European identity. His body was an instrument used in the demarcation of the "other." In this case, the other is taken away from his right, making use of the reduction to identity that is, at the same time, a condemnation to the ghetto: the "same" says the "other," be it the Indian, the beggar, the poor, the prostitute, the children, the women, whatever he wants to say from the point of view of his "identity," of his "sameness" and of what this "identity" means forged "alterity."

This "saying" defines a place to be occupied, a place where the individual is put, as if imprisoned, in a chain whose bonds are only apparently symbolic when compared to his concrete character. For it is the particularity of the other, his condition as a living person oriented in his own way of life established in cultural contexts, which is denied by the identity projected in the other.

Non-identity is that which, in the other, cannot be reduced. It is what does not fit in with hetero-determinations and the very act of conceptualizing. In *On Subject and Object,* Adorno speaks of a "living singular man" (der lebendige Einzelmensh) who would be the incarnation of the *Homo oeconomicus*. We can say that this *Homo oeconomicus* is the figure of transcendental measurement that establishes the "identity" as a rule. It implies the need for "measures." Columbus' interest is all "capital," in the sense of being religious and capitalist, of establishing a "truth" that serves as a measure.

In Adorno's analysis, *Homo oeconomicus* is much more a transcendental subject than the living individual, while one is the victim of the abstract model of exchange. Someone who, as an unknown individual before Columbus, was forcibly introduced into the category used by the transcendental subject: "Indian." This means that the empirical individual is "deformed" by the abstraction of a transcendental subject that precedes him. That one is objectified by a concept that sustains him and that is, himself, previously objectified.

The body of the indigenous man judged from the existence of a soul, thus finding the illegitimate legitimation to be enslaved, is part of the history of the "exploited body." This means that the separation between empirical (a body which is only a body) and transcendental (a body that would have a soul), is already an elaboration of traditional European thought, whose objective is to promote domination by the concrete submission to transcendental. What is transcendental is the idea and the discourse that conveys it, be it from Columbus or from today's disinformation process carried out by media companies and their agents who are acting against the people.

The only way out of this game of submission to the transcendental is to face the construction of the transcendental, to force the transcendental from the concrete, and its applications through a critical path. This implies the consciousness of the construction of the subject and the internal separation of the subject: it is necessary to keep in mind the perspective that, on the one hand, the separation between transcendental and empirical subject is true. Adorno says that "the knowledge of real separation always manages to express the split character of the human condition, something that emerged by force," but, on the other hand, it is false: "separation cannot be hypostatic or transformed into invariant." This means, in concrete terms, that indigenous self-awareness enters history as counter-consciousness knowing that dialogue is impossible, because the other does not want to dialogue with it.

Remembering Homi Bhabha, when talking about the African-American artist Renée Green,[12] there is at stake the need to understand cultural difference as the production of minority identities that 'cleave'— which in themselves are already divided—in the act of articulating a collective body. Only this division is the consciousness of division, an unexpected counter-consciousness to the dominant consciousness.

Preventing the "knowledge" of the other, in Todorov's view of the invaders, is the system of beliefs, the religious and metaphysical truth they represent, but also the economic interest, the "gold" that they seek in these distant lands. There is an interest in general, one might say, crowned by an argument of "authority" that makes travelers manage their belief as if they know what they will find ahead. It is not a question, for these European exploiters, of seeking the truth, but of finding, as Todorov said, "confirmations of a truth known beforehand." Such men traveling at that time began in the name of their knowledge— knowledge supposed by themselves and their culture—a process of "colonization and destruction of others." Knowledge was the excuse for the violence they would carry out in the name of their country's crown, the god of their religion and, to sum up, the truth from their point of view. Columbus was, like all conservatives, an authoritarian subject in whose background the subject of "certainty" was sustained, for whom the "other" is always subjected to the previous truth of his system of beliefs and, as it cannot be otherwise, of the discourse and actions that it sustains.

---

[12] Bhabha, Homi. *The location of culture*. Routledge, 2004.

Todorov insists on the limit of the worldview of the conquerors. In the case of Columbus, it is the limit of his own language. Therefore, he will remain illiterate in the local languages and, at the same time, use the act of "appointment" as a way to take possession of the world around him. In the objects around him—and in people taken as objects—he puts the names he brings with him, without understanding that human communication in the sense of adventure from the point of view of the other, or of dialogue, could be valuable in his journey.

Columbus was a man of speech, not dialogue. And he used language as domination within his epistemological limits. As Todorov rightly notes, he was not successful in communication because he was not interested in it. And that is because, according to their point of view, the "Indians" were just "living objects." According to Todorov's interpretation, Cortez was not as limited as Columbus, for he sought an interpreter as soon as he arrived. However, this would not change Cortez's point of view, since this meeting with the other makes him even more fit for the intended conquest.

For Todorov, however, Cortez will defeat the Aztecs not only because of his strength, but also because the Aztecs "lost control of communication" and thus became weaker. They lost the capacity to interpret the advent of the enemy; they lost the relationship with prophecy, the capacity to interpret the facts. It is almost as if they had lost their own point of view, and were instead crushed by the point of view of the enemy. History is also, we might say, a struggle of speeches and perspectives.

In the war of prospects, Europeans were stronger because they were more violent. They practiced that hermeneutic violence from the point of view of crushing the other, who does not recognize him. That is, they did not project their worldview on the enemy while the enemy projected his on them, weakening them. More object than recipient of a discourse, the "other" was nothing more than a mere thing to be surpassed in a literal sense. If war always depends on a dispute over truths, and truths imply projections, faced with the enemy, the Aztecs lost their relationship with their gods, but more importantly lost the weapon of language and the ability to do violence through it. They were defeated in the identification procedure that is confused with the projection.

What we can say, trying to look on the side of the constitutive lack of these anti-relationships, since they are relations of domination, is that all the conquerors have triumphed by using language in a non-dialogical way. They avoided dialogue, always sustaining, in one way or another, their supposed and imposed "reason" loaded with previous truths. If it is true that the failure of communication is the lack of capacity for dialogue, in this case the defeat of the Aztecs had to do with the fact that "the renunciation of language is the recognition of a defeat," as Todorov states, but only because there was no proposition of dialogue on the part of the oppressor. The power of omen in a super-determined society, as pointed out in Todorov's book, was fundamental, but it only served to annihilate any chance of another role for language.

The fact that Montezuma and his Spanish rapine opponents could not "talk" was decisive. The chance of this conversation never existed in the process of conquest, colonization and catechesis because the principle of identity is not based on dialogue, but on hermeneutic violence: all otherness must be reduced to interpretation from the point of view of the same.

Hermeneutic violence avoids astonishment and strangeness as a positive quality of the other, who is therefore reduced to the exotic. It is a contemporary question which in Todorov, is a statement about the texts of the conquerors: the inexistence of a "radical feeling of strangeness" in the "discovery of other continents and of other men." It is important to see that we have not left the same place on this issue. In Brazil today, the popular perception of native peoples is summarized in exoticism and curiosity on the side of, say, more positive collective perception, and on the negative side, of neglected and hatred.

Besides, there is one more thing that matters to us. Todorov chooses to work on this text with the idea of an "exterior other," one to which the Spanish conquistadors did not relate immediately and which did not contribute to the way they understood the function of language did. The "perception that Spaniards have of Indians" allows us to think that the vision that non-Indians have of Indians today is because we realize that the same lack of dialogue remains. Lack of dialogue is a symptom not only of the absence of recognition but of a violent projection of truth on the other. The role of language is not to communicate, but instead to offer to mere discourse in the name of a single truth.

Upon reflecting carefully, it may sound like a testimonial of stupidity or idiocy that a previous belief system projects this truth. However, if we consider that intelligence is a category of ethics, we need to go a little deeper to understand that it evil exists in the actions of the one who denies the other and that the basis of language usage is always either ethical or unethical.

The other is always a relativistic category. The other constitutes the "same" while, at the same time, the "other" can destroy the "same."

The profound meaning of politics, as well as ethics as the understanding of subjectivity in philosophical terms, depends on the understanding of relationships as established by language. Language can project our truths on to the other or communicate without violence. The relationship developed with the exterior other, as Todorov says, explains something about ourselves, while we are positioning in the place of the "same."

We can, therefore, take the place of the other ourselves. We tend to have a relationship of exoticism with the other. The exotic is always the foreigner, is the one that, in our mental-cultural habit and by common sense, we always try to lead to what we already know. The "principle of identity"—this mania of reducing what is alien into customary—inflicts harm in our knowledge process. Its result is a kind of betrayal in which the same becomes an enemy of the other, who would like to make an enemy. The knowledge that is eliminating by understanding the space of "between us."

Reading the anthropologist Viveiros de Castro, it seems, however, that it is more than necessary to bring to the table a "reshaping of the conceptual charts."[13] Viveiros de Castro proposes the relationship between what he and others call "perspectivism" as well as what he calls "multinaturalism" that is a kind of "cosmic politics." We see a substantial change in the relationship between them that affects the almost absolute sense that the term recognition has reached in the tradition of European philosophy. That allows us to question it in terms of its objectivity. At stake, it is no longer a "same" and an "other"; but in the context of a "general economy of otherness," he searches the

---

[13] Viveiros de Castro, Eduardo. *A inconstância da alma selvagem*. São Paulo: Cosacnaify, 2006.

multiplicity of points of view, like a real "mobility" of "points of view" that are not based on something like a principle of identity.

Something like a general "relationality" or "relativity" is what presents itself in Viveiros de Castro's thought, limiting the reach of categories like "same" and "other" in the context of "recognition." The "indiscrimination between humans and animals" makes one think of the general change in what can be understood. Another metaphysics that is not metaphysical at all is on the scene, displacing the issues of nature and culture, "humanity" and "animality" into a great indistinctness—an "integrally relational ontology"—among all the things that participate in the same soul in the world. The question of points of view remains, but they assume another facet. The points of view are different, depending on the bodily forms of beings, no more than a principle of identity which oppose each other, but establish them in general relativity. In the words of Viveiros de Castro: "This is the concept, common to many peoples of the continent, according to which the world is inhabiting by different species of subjects or people, human and non-human, who perceive it from different points of view." Viveiros de Castro poses the problem of "seeing how" animals see humans and humans see animals, and beings in general see each other.

If we can apply here a general summary of the question: If the notion of "subject" were on the scene, it would not simply imply that of a projected "object." If we can say that "same" and "other" are no longer pertinent in the "epistemological game" of "objectification," the "Other" of the Amerindians, is no longer something simply relative to the same. It persists in the form of "person" in an expansive sense of subjectivation. Its character is no longer a thing that resists in the opposition between nature and culture, but in the indiscernibleness with nature in which the pattern "subject vs object" ceases to matter.

Instead of ethnocentrism, which can always be attributed to peoples in general, cosmocentrism emerges from the Amerindians as an advanced posture in general ecological terms including in regard to the human condition.

Paranoia and Self-Referentiality

Columbus discovered the Native Americans, but didn't care about them. He was not interested in understanding their language. He named them "Indians" due to a mistake—a "nominative furor," as Todorov says—that he never intended to clarify.

He analyzed his interlocutors according to their Christian faith, their understanding of governmental hierarchy, and his fantasy of the exotic. According to Todorov, who understood Columbus' attitude as an action of an "idiot", he sought confirmation of his ideas rather than the truth.

We are not different from Columbus. To this day, more than 500 years after the start of the indigenous genocide that has not yet ceased, we suffer from the same nominative furor, the same mania for identification. Five hundred years later, this mania became old-fashioned. It was already obsolete in 1492, more than 1,500 years after it arose in Greek philosophy. Such a mania is, in fact, the paranoia of self-reference that constitutes the basic pattern—the aristocratic basis of knowledge that is not perceived as foreign—of a way of understanding the world.

In other words, the inevitability of "who we are" is what makes us interpret the world one way or another. If we do not make space to understand that the stranger also inhabits us, we close windows to the diversity of life implied in the possibility of knowing. The ideal of identity still used today in certain discourses and humanities research has become a real weapon against understanding, by promising the explanation of all the difference (a word often used to designate identity).

To identify, that is, to bring the exterior into oneself, is an inexorable mental fact. However, it can be rethinking in the direction of ethical knowledge, which involves respect for different things until the implosion of the procedure of devouring identification of the alterity.

What is at stake is the reduction of the other to an object. The problem is the inability to see the other as a subject in law, a subject who has "the same" rights. The reduction of the other human subject to object occurs in the fallacious strategy of reducing identity when it is saying that the other "is" this or that. By saying that the other is "Indian" while "I am not," I guarantee the truth of the opposition by creating a collective identity for the other, composed of diverse individuals. In his analysis of Orientalism, Edward Said realized that this construction of the identity of the other has "murderous efficacy," which leads us to think of the proposition of genocide as a transcendental constitutive element of every discourse that constructs the "identification" of the other while he is the "framing" of the other.

To understand and modify this situation is the historical task that belongs to every intellectual, researcher, teacher, or student, artist or writer, who does not merely wish to close their eyes to the violence and barbarism of our time.

4

The Effort of Dialogue

Reflective thinking should help us overcome this fascist moment that threatens the world. The ethical impulse that drives this book is in that possibility. What I am calling dialogue, or "dialogue," can bring us hope. Dialogue is not just a form of philosophy, rather philosophy in its pure state. Dialogue is the attitude that can alter the spiritual and material conditions in which fascism arises. Furthermore, we must not imagine that there are secure solutions to defeat fascism. Our engagement should, therefore, keep in mind that dialogue is not an easy task.

Our life is structuring in language on a conscious and unconscious level. There is the field of the symbolic, the imaginary and the real, what everyone knows, what we think we know and what we do not know because we do not want to know: the place where our primitive fears reside.

Everything is, however, language or something that refers to it. Philosophy is one of its most important events because, as a careful thought, it helps us think beyond the immediate aspects of life, beyond the dogmas that we often accept for lack of sensitivity and attention to thought processes as language processes. There is no event more important than language and more philosophical than dialogue. However, the dialogue is neither a chat nor a simple conversation.

Those who have read Plato[1] believe that the heart of dialogue cannot be writing, that the text known in Plato's thinking is a vehicle for memory. However, the text presents us with staging, not the totality of the memory. Neither is it the most fundamental part. Plato said that philosophy was the dialogue of the soul with itself. Moreover, the soul cannot be put on paper, although the text can be the vehicle that leads to it.

Reflection depends on dialogue, which is an intricate work, and dialogue depends on reflection. Just as Hegel spoke of an "effort of the concept," today we must speak of an effort of dialogue. However, what is dialogue? Dialogue is not a discursive form, nor performativity of any kind, precisely because it is not a ready-made text. Dialogue can be transformed into text only after it takes place as Plato showed us in his various dialogues. No one can predict anything about the dialogic event. Where there is foresight, there is speech. Dialogue is the creative form of language created in a deep formulation that escapes the text.

The language that constitutes us is the language we use every day to communicate and express ourselves. "Living together," to remember Roland Barthes,[2] is always complicated, and only dialogue leads us to the construction of experience of recognition to which we call democracy. It is true that, in society, "language games" work.

---

[1] I recommend reading the Phaedrus, which deals specifically with dialogue, but also with the Theaetetus, the Cratylus, Meno and various other Plato's dialogues that also present methodological issues.

[2] *Comment vivre ensemble: Courses and seminars at the Collège de France (1976–1977)*, Seuil, 2002.

Nevertheless, the dialogue is how language goes beyond the mechanics of a game. Dialogue builds the "common" as a dance between creative subjects and those who recognize themselves in their rights.

Fascism is a language game that can be faced by another language game. Fascism is the mechanical and self-destructive game of sad emotions, such as hatred and envy, against the original game of love and gratitude.[3] The game of serious and attentive bethinking in dialogical processes goes beyond the game of power that is under most different language games. What matters now is the difference between the game and the toy.

Politics has been turning into a power game. That contributed to increasing hatred for it. People may hate politics precisely because they have already placed high hopes on it. People have been frustrated, because the process of politics has disappeared and only the power games remain. Only by bethinking, we are capable of facing that. However, how can we advance bethinking if we are in the midst of all kinds of fundamentalism? Are we in the middle of a period of obscurantism?

Philosophy, in this context, is a form of systematic dialogue, whether with another concrete person, an interlocutor, a friend, or just someone who is willing to exercise thinking. Dialogue also happens with books and their authors. We often talk more with our favorite authors than with our family members. That is not a mistake or a flaw. In order to establish dialogue, the soul must be present, and this does not usually occur in conversation, but rather in silence. We do not always feel

---

[3] I suggest the lecture of Melanie Klein: *Envy and Gratitude and other works 1946-1963*. Vintage Classics, 1996.

comfortable sharing our deepest thoughts with those we are closest to in everyday life. We can overcome this, but it takes the effort of dialogue to reach the other person. However that does not merely mean that someone has to talk to everyone or all the time.

Nowadays, it is necessary to seek an exercise in philosophy "with" people. It is necessary to insist on a "common philosophy"[4] that is not merely a search for consensus. In a dialogue, we are not in a theater; neither are we in search of consensus. We are getting ready to find the truth. The courage of dialogue implies living with and recognizing differences.

Dialogue does not arise to create consensus or to avoid the struggle for hegemony that we seek. The struggle for hegemony is the struggle for what Hegel called the "struggle for recognition." The search for consensus is a modest use of dialogue, but a simple conversation can solve the problem of consensus. The purpose of dialogue is not to standardize ways of thinking and speeches in the service of interest. The effort of dialogue is the effort of difference. It is equivalent to the method that keeps us alive as thinking beings.

Dialogue is a type of psychosocial resistance, which holds the power of social transformation at its most structuring level—shaping dialogue matters when we want a democratic society. The democracy we want cannot be the illusion that we are all equal. Rights must be guaranteed and, in order to achieve this, capitalism as an anti-dialogical system must be dismantled. None of this will be possible if we do not recreate ties based on dialogue.

---

[4] Years ago, I wrote a book with this title in an attempt to explain the method of dialogue: *Philosophy in Common, Filosofia em Comum*. Record, 2008.

We need to foment the subjectivity that creates dialogue and the dialogue that creates subjectivity. We need to invent this hermeneutic circle, as there will be no democracy without dialogue if we do not know that dialogue is defined as exchange and coexistence between differences. The significant contribution of philosophy and the human sciences to this age in which authoritarianism grows and develops without limits is the production of dialogue as the production of recognition.

Dialogue is the specific form of philosophy as a practice, or as activism. It is not a mere chat, a walk-off game, no matter how pleasurable such activities may be. Dialogue is the sensitive and concrete life of democracy. Democracy that safeguards rights and prevents violence is threatening in all areas of culture, institutions and daily life precisely because of the absence of dialogue. In this sense, the role of teachers, thinkers, researchers and intellectuals in general in the transformation of society toward better material living conditions, which includes rights, also implies helping to improve emotional and subjective conditions through access to qualified thinking, education and art.

No coexistence will be peaceful and respectful, and no society will be better if the hallucinated element, the dementia of fascism of which Adorno spoke, is not stopped. Fascism grows due to the absence of cognitive and intellectual work. We need an education for democracy that is education for art and poetry, for science and critical thinking. We need education beyond capital.[5]

---

[5] Mészáros, István. *A Educação para Além do Capital*. São Paulo: Boitempo Editorial, 2005.

The demands of social transformation challenge critical thinking and the work of intellectuals in all areas, demanding attitude. The intellectual class runs the risk of losing its ethical-political place if it seeks an image of neutrality in the face of facts. When we see the current advance of neoliberal fascism over public universities around the world, against education, we understand why engagement is necessary. Serious thinking is not neutral: either it is the confirmation of the state of things, or it is critical and transforming. Every social transformation implies the transformation of subjectivities toward lucid thinking intertwined with lucid practices in our obscurantist times.

If our political being is formed by acts of language, we need to consider this when the impoverishment caused by fascism is becoming so clear. Authoritarianism is the system of impoverishment. Fascism is the name given to this extremist moment when fascism manages to touch the masses and influence their thoughts, feelings and attitudes. Authoritarianism implies the impoverishment of political acts caused by the interruption of dialogue. An interruption that occurs, in turn, due to the destruction of the conditions in which dialogue could take place: free thinking, education and cultivation of the arts. These conditions are material and concrete. There are mechanisms, in the form of habit-creating devices, that impede dialogue. These are created by rationalities that operate in language by imposing or manipulating formulas. This movement of working rationalities can be called a "game." The game is not creative per se; it is the formula within which players work. Furthermore, we play many games unconsciously.

Language is outside, and inside us, it shapes us while, at the same time, it is forged by us. Language is the environment where we are, where we become beings in action, as Simone de Beauvoir said, or beings in "performance," that is, beings who act in front of others and who, overcoming the performance, learn to dialogue. Once dialogue takes place, of course, we can see in it something performative. At the same time, there is something that escapes performance: the element of surprise, the uncommon and mysterious that is the power of dialogue in our lives.

Dialogue is an activity that forms us and is formed by us. It is a complex linguistic act capable of promoting actions of transformation at different levels, whether personal or collective. It is, above all, the ethical-political way of being in a language environment. We must ask ourselves what happens to us when we join the dialogue. What happens when dialogue is necessary and, yet, not possible? Dialogue is a practice of non-violence. Violence arises when dialogue does not come into play.

Ethics and Subjectivity— A Dialogical Question

The relationship we have with otherness implies the "psychological" element of our political experiences of our life in common. At this point, we should talk about ethics. Ethics concerns precisely the psychological sphere formerly called "morals." Ethics signal to the "other" as part of the moral dimension. At the level of language work, it is the dialogue that sustains ethics. We currently use the term "ethics" to talk about this issue, and we use "morals" in the sense of habits and customs, as what comes to be questioned through ethics. When I ask how someone is formed, how someone becomes who they are, I am in the sphere of ethics as an instance of thinking on the action of becoming someone.

The linguistic action par excellence is dialogue. What is at stake when we talk about otherness is the subjective experience of people who meet and join a dialogical process. We are referring to the way of being of each place formed by an encounter with the other. Subjectivity is the result of an encounter with otherness. Subjectivity will be narrower if it is less open to otherness. What would be the difference in the bond between a person and someone that seems to represent "otherness" and the bond that a person has with an authoritarian, fascist leader or a group with fascist characteristics? Do we all need each other? Do we all need emotional and group bonding? We can and should always ask ourselves from Freud,[6] what makes certain people bind themselves to authoritarianism?

I use the word subjectivity to express what is proper to each one, but also the field of "common" psychic and moral organized from an emotional bond (*Gefühlsbindungen*) that we can treat as being an ideological bond. In my opinion, we need to bear in mind the notion of the emotional bond exposed in Freud's text about the psychology of the masses as one of the most important to understand how fascism reaches people.

By the word subjectivity, I also mean what everyone feels and lives in their skin. I am referring to those experiences that are independent

---

[6] In his book of 1921, Freud asked himself what happened to people so that they would give themselves to the masses, what was the mental transformation lived by people in the masses ("seelische Wandlung des Einzelnen in der Masse"). In Freud, Sigmund. *Jenseits des Lustprinzips / Massenpsychologie und Ich-Analyse / Das Ich und das Es: Und andere Werke aus den Jahren 1920–1924*. Fischer, 1998.

of us, and that touches us positively or make us suffer at different levels. It is about the psychosocial stuff we are made of. The term "interiority" could also be applied here, but it would not be enough to speak of a simple interior experience, because subjectivity also implies "exteriority." It concerns the body. It implies what is happening around us and what transcends what we can understand.

We cannot always understand what happens to us. We are part of history, as actors and as victims, what is happening to us is something perpetrated by the other, not just the physical person of the other. What makes us who we are—institutions, society, culture, and the spiritual and symbolic realm? Moreover, what are we? We are unfinished beings; we are beings in the process, beings whose quality is to seek understanding. Besides, for this to be possible, we need to learn to look at each other and understand how they have a relationship of precedence over us. When we arrived in the world, it was because the other one was already there.

That is why the question, "What are we doing with each other?" is so important. It concerns the field of otherness, the ability to find the other in oneself, but also the ability to open oneself emotionally to the mystery of the other who is not in me. In our society, empathy as in the absence of prejudices is low, as is compassion[7] as the possibility of feeling the suffering of others. They challenge us to build a space-time and an everyday life of another quality. For this to be possible, it is necessary to overthrow capitalism. Nevertheless, there is no point in overthrowing capitalism outside ourselves if we do not eliminate the

---

[7] Schopenhauer, Arthur. *The Two Fundamental Problems of Ethics*. Cambridge: Cambridge University Press, 2009.

subjective and relational conditions that keep it active as a rationality of the human world.

In the same way, the issue is also to think of the political act as an ethical act, and as a linguistic act (every linguistic act is political). And to ask what we are doing when we are saying things to each other in the sense of the performativity of the language and about ethics involved in it.

In this context, potential fascism concerns the inability to ask this question about the world around us. It would be ethical to find room for that question. The space for this question implies a fundamental ethical-political space that is also poetic-political.

A Theoretical–Practical Experiment

When I wrote the first essay that gave this book its name, I thought of a theoretical–practical experiment. I thought about how to trigger the nearly impossible action to talk to someone who is hardening in his or her worldview. Someone who is not willing to listen? Someone who does not react to dialogue instead to command and dominate. Someone who became the priest of the truths of their own lives and those of others? Someone who knows everything beforehand and is closest to the other? As lost in a personal island, some people are delighted that things cannot be different because the world is ready in their paranoid thinking systems, full of precious truths. Thinking systems are now language systems. The core of conservative thinking, which is tendentially oppressive, is in a linguistically stiffened mental backdrop. We can think in a backdrop in which the authoritarian subject camouflages like a moth which defends itself against predators. The truth for all those who incarnate authoritarianism, and it is proof that, deep down, as in any paranoid system, one is not free from fear.

Someone, who thinks that, in the other, life, society cannot be different, does not open himself to dialogue. There as is an idealizing and utopian dimension in every dialogue. However, the fascist does not care about that or even analyze this hypothesis. The other, this "someone" that the fascist agent treats as "no one" is something too different for their head full of ready-made ideas and will fit in the same place as always.

Fascism is a form of radical authoritarianism. There is this power in every State because "order" in itself, the order proper to the State, is the essence of fascism. In everyday life, authoritarianism survives in psychic or morally rigid postures and attitudes. The coldness of postures, thoughts and actions, is, deep within, the food of potential fascism. All our inability to love in one sense that values the other is the source of fascism.

We detach ourselves from talking and are incapable of creating a different ethical–political scenario. The other, the one we treat as nobody, is the ethical-political challenge in a society that works for the guarantee of fundamental rights and respect for uniqueness. The challenge of the other as the challenge of difference is what we have to take forward.

The authoritarianism of everyday life is a domestic and social issue at the same time. It is important to stress the domestic issue as a territory of various forms of violence. Fascism in the domestic sphere also concerns machismo, and the forms of violence suffered mainly by women and children. We cannot forget that machismo has been an ally of fascism throughout its history. Moreover, I would even say they inspire each other.

In our time, manifestations of racial, ethnic, religious and sexual prejudice, which we thought had been overcome, are growing in all spheres of life. Related to the right wing and to the left wing, from all faiths, from all defenses that should be the fairest and generous. At the same time, that brutal idiosyncrasies assert themselves against people and groups, socially necessary feelings, those who turn to the other in order to understand them, to welcome them—in a word, to love them—have no place among authoritarian personalities. The most basic openness to conversation becomes unfeasible when individuals are locked in their small, previously formed, and informed universes regarding all they suppose they know.

For centuries we have been trained to say that "power corrupts." It is a cliché that we have never questioned. Speech by imitation is based on the repetitive and banal quotation. Authoritarianism is "citationalist." It repeats ideas launched in the field of fascist propaganda, itself vicious and repetitive. Authoritarianism depends on its repeatability. Authoritarianism is a machine of unconscious production of a subjectivity deformed by discourse. Hence, the importance of hates speech. We do not think about what we say. To understand the content of what we say, we need to understand the way we say it. That is very complicated.

Dialogue is the reason why we do not pay attention to what can be a dialogue, itself a way of talking full of powers and which is easily cancelled if we do not insist on it. We do not experience it in everyday microphysics, where it could be said to be about power of transformation in macrophysical terms. Dialogue between the singular and the general—between what we are (or want to be) and what surrounds us—would serve us well.

Experimentum Crucis

Let us make a theoretical–practical experimentum crucis with this highly metaphorical question that we have to bethink on fascism. Can we treat the question as an interrogation and try to answer it pragmatically? "How do you talk to a fascist?". I say this thinking that we can move beyond the discourse of denunciation or complaint that are protoforms of criticism. Is is interesting, emphasize the "how" operator and move on.

Let us put our fragility in the middle of the way to face fascism. Let us remember that we are all potential victims. I am thinking now of the type of hate speech, which, through the attack, and through strategies of humiliation, positions us as victims. There are the deadly victims, those for whom, according to Benjamin, there is no justice. We must ask ourselves the question of the victims who remain alive, and the issue of potential victims who are all people who exist under fascist regimes. It is terrifying to ask such a question when we think that all those who remain devoted to democracy are potential victims of fascism. Just as there are potential fascists in diverse gradations, so the potential victims are diverse. Evidently not all are the same, just as suffering is not the same.

When we talk about fascism, we are talking about an imminent danger. If there is the fascist in a state of readiness, anyone who fits the paranoid pattern can be a victim. Fascism is just as serious and even more so when we treat it tritely. And yet it is us, the potential victims, us who remain alive, who must fight against fascism. So we are not only current or potential victims of fascism, but also beings in a state of resistance.

Fascism survives in animosity. Now, whoever is attacked in everyday life in the discursive and practical positions of fascism cannot cancel himself out in the position of victim. We do not leave the position of potential victims when we fight. When we enter the position of struggle, we become different from the executioners. If those who are potential victims do not fight against their tormentors, they are in danger of becoming equal to them.

The victim's position is of impotence. It is a dangerous position in itself. It does not guarantee protection from the law, even though it is possible to denounce the inequality and violence to which one is subjected in a society whose logic is exclusion. However, the position of victim cannot function as a "strategy" for survival in times when power is in perverse hands, which aim to immolate victims on the altar of the State that serves Capital. Victim status as a strategy can become a trap. Fascism itself has transformed the condition of victim into a trap: the victimism used as a strategy by the fascists—for instance, when white supremacy claims to be oppressed—is the issue we must face.

Let us take seriously what Adorno said: "The victim awakens the desire to proscribe."[8] If the system of power, if the religion of capitalism, implies the previous guilt of the other,[9] if the "useless people" are previously marked by simply existing, it is because they were previously guilty. The question of life that does not deserve to be

[8] Adorno, Theodor Wiesengrund and Horkheimer, Max. *Dialektik der Aufklärung. Philosophische Fragmente.* In: Adorno, Theodor W. *Gesammelte Werke*, Vol. 3. Frankfurt am Main: Suhrkamp, 1997.

[9] Benjamin, Walter. Kapitalismus als Religion. [Fragment], in: *Gesammelte Schriften*, Hrsg.: Rolf Tiedemann und Hermann Schweppenhäuser, 7 Bde, Frankfurt am Main: Suhrkamp, 1. Auflage, 1991, Bd. VI, S. 100–2.

lived is now presented. Those who "should not exist" are guilty if they exist. And if they are guilty, they are condemned. Assuming the position of victim who is confused with the position of the guilty in our capitalist society is to expose oneself and, as a result, to open the flank to the massacre. Women know how this works; they are accused of being guilty when they suffer violence such as rape. There is a macho rationality that is mistaken for fascism and exterminates what is different.

Instead of the position of victim, used by fascists who victimize themselves, we can think of another position. It would be like the subtle posture of the warrior and the conceptual guerrilla, the one who assumes a kind of careful and delicate struggle and challenges power from within, from its hard core, to dismantle it radically. I speak of this because the direct, physical confrontation tends to take the lives of those who find themselves in the hardest trenches—on the streets, for example. The point is, we can't let the "snake's egg" release its hatchlings. In tense situations, when the train of history threatens to skid, it is necessary to use the handbrake.

What subtle guerrilla 3 are we talking about? If power is "phallogocentric," that is, phallic and works in the context of discursiveness, it is necessary to face this power by disarming the discursive and practical "devices" that structure it. Adorno spoke of psychoanalysis and education, but we also need to strengthen the art against machismo, racism and xenophobia for a culture of recognition. This culture of recognition will not be possible in the context of capitalism. If power does not sustain dialogue, and even prevents it and avoids it, the issue would be, for instance, to intensify it.

Dialogue at all levels is undesirable in authoritarian systems. Authoritarian personalities don't cultivate dialogue; they're incapable of it. However, dialogue as we have been discussing it since the beginning of this book, is not just a conversation, much less a conversation in which an argument is disputed. Dialogue is the opposite of speech—and only dialogue can disarm speech. Only dialogue can remove the device from power without becoming a new consensus device.

I use the term device[10] here in Foucault's sense, that is, as the complex mechanism which works by reproducing what is given. Dialogue is a counter-device whose fundamental capacity is to avoid the constitution of devices of power. Nevertheless how can a dialogue be carried out if the dialogue at its concrete level implies at least two free wills? When only one is willing to engage in dialogue, what role does the one who does not care about dialogue play? This does not mean that dialogue does not make a difference, rather that dialogue becomes impotent and limited precisely due to its "disempowerment." But what do we need in order to get to dialogue? Do we need "dialogue" to get to "dialogue," after all? In that case, the dialogue would be a petition of principle marked by a vicious circle, a simple tautology?

Are the conditions for dialogue to be constructed or would dialogue be the condition for political existence? The fact that we are language beings who establish politics in its most original condition from the bonds that are established by language, allows us to think that dialogue is neither simply a before nor simply an afterthought.

---

[10] Foucault, Michel. *A microfísica do Poder*. Paz e Terra, 2000.

Dialogue is precisely the way of being human. And the problem, in this case, would not be to establish dialogue as a technology (which would only serve to seek consensus), but to think of dialogue as a habitus, in the sense of Bourdieu.[11] In the sense of a simple political technology uprooted from the world of life, it is clear that we cannot "talk to fascists," but we can and must create a new habitus, that of dialogue, so that there are no more grounds for fascism.

What mechanisms do we have to win the fight against fascist violence? Under what conditions is fascism born? What devices do those who fight for something that can be called humanity and civilization against barbarism have at their disposal? Can we act without counting power devices? I am proposing dialogue as a counter-device, not as a technology. Dialogue as a methodology, as a propositional practice.

Rights advocates know that talking to hardened personalities is impossible. Dialogue, however, would need to be transformed into methodology. Just as psychoanalysis is not just a conversation, but a method based on language analysis, dialogue is the philosophical method that should become a political methodology until it becomes a habit.

Dialogue as a habit is stolen from us daily. The philosophical task of our time involves giving it back to people. Our survival as citizens depends on the possibility of perforating the fascist armor—a society of walls built on authoritarian parameters—through a society built on dialogue.

---

[11] Bourdieu, Pierre. *Outine of a theory of practice*. Cambridge: Cambridge University Press, 1977.

Dialogue is, in this case, the basic "democratic methodology" that can operate in private or public situations. Dialogue seems powerless in the face of hatred. It seems too delicate. Dialogue itself is a challenge. Micropolitical challenges can help us think about what to do and how to act on a macropolitical scale.

We are, at that point, in the field of a theoretical–practical strategy. As a way of ensuring that subjectivity survives, I propose that we focus on the challenge from three angles: 1. Let us take into account that the time of the other is a haunted time. It is a frightening time where the other considers that the interlocutor represents the unknown, someone threatens in some sense "my" reality, my order; 2. It is necessary to open up to the time of the other. Opening up one's self to experience is an opening to that haunting that the other causes in us. This requires perceiving oneself as another, which only happens in the imaginary and cognitive discernment. We will never have access to the feeling and thinking of the other, just as they will never have access to who we are. We need to be exposing what we feel and think, which does not happen without linguistic mediation, that is, without expression and careful communications; 3. We are willing to an endless time, to an endless process until the change of our way of being, the production of a new *habitus*. That is, the permanence in the experience of dialogue that serves as a basis for other social and interpersonal relationships. In other words, in order for dialogue to take place, it is necessary to remain in the time-place of dialogue. To insist on the act of listening and speaking in order to make oneself heard in the context of the encounter. To insist on the production of a spirituality, a mentality, a sensitivity that escapes violence. The qualification of the dialogue by insisting on itself demonstrates its pacifist consistency.

It is necessary to say something about listening. The difference between speech and dialogue matters to us here. Dialogue is not a conversation between people that think as equals; it is not just a complementary conversation or a friendly conversation. We do not see dialogue as framing of a consensus, but the real practice of listening. In this sense, the dialogue is a complex adventure in the unknown. It is a real political act between differences that evolve in the search for knowledge and the action that derives from it.

The crucial meaning of "How to talk to a fascist" becomes, on the contrary, an experimental democratic imperative that must be anticipating in the conduct of those who want to produce democracy today. "How to talk to a fascist" is a philosophical experiment of ethical-aesthetic inspiration. There is a logical dimension in this experiment. The operator "how" is a performative function that implies the potential to be affected by a scenic act in the sense of Brecht, who sought to deconstruct and produce consciousness through his socially critical pieces.

Instead of complaining about the lack of openness, we should think about how it can be produced. How can we show the experience of the alterity toward people in avoiding the other? How can we introduce someone to the experience of otherness? A didactic-political and an aesthetic-political approach may be relevant in terms of theoretical–practical design. Unfortunately, we do not have conventional institutions acting in this direction. The institutions (school, Church, family, the state and its powers) deny the other and deny procedures that promote real and concrete encounters. It would be necessary to apply displacement policies—that would make us think and act in transformative directions—to shake the established scenario and the subjectivities that sustain it.

We, therefore, need to change the institutions or create institutions capable of contemplating the other. Lèvi-Strauss spoke of "openness to the other" as a characteristic of the Amerindian peoples, as opposed to their colonizers. We should exercise that potential.

The Digital Misadventure

Digital life transforms the other into a spectrum. Its concrete, analogical dimension disappears. In the digital age, we touch everything with our fingertips; the body is a remote memory, as is existence. Inhibited in ourselves, but forgotten of the body where we are isolated, we do not have any desire to sail with improvised rafts to explore the waters around the island. Adventure is not our goal in security time at any cost. But we are committed to the digital adventure, because it does not present us with threats.

The digital adventure becomes the only one possible. In front of the computer, people feel safe, just as we feel safe in front of the television screen. Security is an illusion, but the illusion of security is enough. The global security agencies, as well as the agencies that steal our data, know where we are and, if we remain in agreement, no one will suffer much from the subtle theft practiced by dishonest companies.

No one escapes. However who would really like to run away? Seduction bought most people in the great system of virtual power where everyone wants to have their piece of land in the great latifundium of cyberspace. We live happy with what we can have: easy simulations always provide everything we want. Standing still, we receive what we think we need and do not question ourselves about our actions. At the same time, we live under the abstract praise of "practice." The daily digital act solves every problem we may have. The digital act, the one that makes us confirm our presence in an event to which we have not always been invited, and which does not always require real presence, an event organized in digital networks, is the act of our virtual age. The digital act allows us to buy with a "click" without having a close look at the item to be purchased or even needing that item. The digital act that makes us flirt, make sex and even fall in love with digital sincerity with people that we have never seen. What I call a digital act is the new form of act that replaces any performance. The simulation of life is the new way of living.

On our own island, we can live with digital acts. We are more and more alone, because when we talk too much, without having anything to say, we are always talking to ourselves. On the other side there is someone, who is also lost on their own island. They scream trying to make themselves heard. We don't worry much about listening because, in addition to being hard working, the one who screams sounds more like a madman. And listening to them promises to be very boring. Well, everything we already know sounds boring. However, what we do not know scares us if we are also focused on the security of our ready thoughts, as if this security were confused with being in the same place. And we send messages, as if we were shouting at the other, that someone we treat as "nobody," as if they were there to listen to us. We don't listen to them, but they will certainly listen to us—that's what our fantasy assures us. I mean, our island is also the center of the world and everything around us serves to buy this costume. I fantasize, so I exist.

I stand in front of the computer and act digitally. Inaction suits me. I feel like a person from my time acting like this with my fingertips. Without moving, I act without acting. Inertia is the protective function of life. Conservatism by inaction, is our great achievement nowadays. It is hidden under the digital act that gives us deep impression of accomplishment. In fact, it does a lot of things, but it changes the quality of existence.

Many of us feel lost; we are adrift in the immense sea of the Internet where we surf. The metaphor of navigation has long been used to understand what the Internet is. Social networks are like boats that lead go nowhere. Our messages on social networks are like those bottles thrown into the sea in the hope that someone will find them and save us from our perdition. We get used to living adrift in virtual life and with the certainty that no other life is possible, a certainty that generates accommodation. We get used to drifting because, paradoxically, although it is made up of total uncertainty, it brings us a guarantee: we do not need to go anywhere, we do not need to go out of ourselves.

However, we still feel lost. Furthermore, only because we are stuck on our island. Moreover, let us not wish otherwise. It is quite possible that the bottle thrown to the sea does not have the objective of communicating with anyone. Does the bottle have only one end? Or is it just a plastic bottle thrown out of carelessness. It is there just because everyone does that of throwing bottles into the sea, and it no longer serves for them to find us. We throw many bottles into repetitive and compulsive gestures. It may even be that we somehow realize in our un-realization.

It is possible that this isolation, that the prison on our particular island, is the place where we want to stay. It can be something comfortable, which, in the extreme, leads us to conservatism. It may be that bottles at sea are just tools for maintaining this state of affairs. Furthermore, it gives the impression that randomly launched communication does not need content. When it is worth communicating, when what was half-finished comes to an end, then everyone has to stop and ask if they are deceiving themselves.

If we think a little more, we will see that in the range of emotions between hatred and love that we experience on a daily basis, in the depths of the insurmountable anguish, there is despair. One kind of desperation in an absolute state that admits no hope. It does not allow us to live a pleasant experience with the inevitable drift, and that wears the mask of speech so as not to be seen. Looking at the despair would be even more desperate. The drift we experience is, therefore, even stranger because there is an island that is always available. We can be comfortable in ourselves, where we already are. Our desire was interrupted by the offer of a ready world, and that is what causes us despair. Despair is not an absence of hope, but desire.

Deep down, it is this firm ground, this certainty of something that attracts us on the island of ourselves. What was promised with transcendence is pure immanence. It is increasingly lowered to merchandise. What is promised in religion, or in consumption—itself religious—in the life of goods and experiences that can be bought is a leap to happiness. It is confused with the values of unquestioned security and promoted as a pure function of repetition. The function of repetition is to avoid questioning.

Moreover, if we avoid questioning, we deny too much. We avoid the transformative conversation that is dialogue. Within this general framework, isolation amid a community is the formula of what is experienced today in social and political terms.

Instead of sailing on a piece of shattered wood on which we cross the sea one day; instead of floating to any land in sight as in the shipwreck stories we have heard, what we do—in our managed and organized drift—is, at best, to take a suspicious turn on our own beaches. It so happens that we have never been inside ourselves, except for the imprisonment on our island. The adventure of going beyond us, the adventure that would be in the order of desire, when it seems possible, does not go far. The island of the neo-Pentecostal shopping mall or church, always depending on the social and cultural class to which it belongs, offers security to the lives that have totally lost the desire to invent themselves.

Cell phones and computers have become oars that take us nowhere. Branded clothes are fashionable, like fashionable cars. They are like rafts that take us to that mythological type of island of the dead that appears in fantasy films. The things we can acquire in the domain of purchasing power are anchors through which we want to feel that we are crossing firm ground, even if we are floating on the high seas, all this without leaving the shores of ourselves. There is an atmosphere of hyper emotion in the air. Today's superficial and hysterical emotion hides a deep coldness in most relationships; themselves mediated by all that is technological, mechanical and cold. The only hope trapped us on the island a long time ago. Although today we talk so much about nomadism and practise it in virtual (and touristic) terms, there is the despair of where to sail on the open sea. Dropping anchor on a familiar known island becomes the real goal. Paradoxically, the adventure has become a commodity, and no-one goes anywhere any more. What attracts the most in the merchandise, the certainty that someone has something, is nothing more than high fantasy.

Despair lies in the fact that no anchor touches the ground, and nothing helps us to achieve or desired level of security or certainty. Nevertheless, that is right that; a pleasant illusion is maybe even better than reality. The metaphor of the island makes us know that, at least, we can count on this safe piece of ground that means staying in the same place with our desires controlled or "colonized" by the propaganda that leads us to consume. It is the fantasy of the firm ground. We complete each other as if our entire search in life were resolved in ourselves. It is just that, actually, maybe in our time, there is no real search for reality and truth. We are not impressed to think that the existence of each one is an end in itself. Since we are isolated, we believe that this is only true for us.

In somewhat more complicated words, "transcendence in the form of immanence" has become sufficient. If we use another metaphor, we can say we follow with the brush in our hands. We are hanging over nothing—no floor at all.

Mechanical Speaking

Taking all that into account, it is not absurd to think that we are talking to ourselves. At the same time, it is clear that we talk to each other. However, the anguish about our acts of language signals the lack of something. The conversations themselves are marked by something inconceivable.

The unspoken is everywhere, and we use speech to cover it up. The unspoken is terrifying. And since we speak of the metaphor of navigation, and we think of these neighboring but always "isolated" islands, silence would be like one of those mythical maritime monsters feared by all, who a few would venture to seek and, if they found it, would be devoured by it. We lack the silence that would allow openness to the other.

Between one island and another where there should be bridges, there are all kinds of debris: plastic remains, ruins, old devices, televisions, telephones, cars, films, computers, the result of all kinds of advertising. Old and new contents and shapes are floating in the sea of life that are objects filling the space between us. Those objects are noisy things. Moreover, we get used to noise because it is our way of living today in times of meaningless speech.

In a culture of noise, the part of silence, if on one side is terrifying, the other seems simply unnecessary. Talking has the rhythm of machines, of mechanical technologies. It is like we have introjected a way of being artificial. The scenery of the islands that we all are is marked by a landscape that is not only visual, but also loud and where it seems that nobody is able to say things that really make sense. Or that it is not possible to listen to what the other person wants to tell us, because we are unprepared for the meaning of others.

We shout desperately at someone on the other side of our island, someone who can't hear us and when we say something that could allow real communication—that which would free us from insulation—we don't find anyone who will listen. However, we don't like this cry made of silence and we continue in the repetitive and disjointed speech that deludes us that we are in deep communication.

Thus, in the rhythm of the conversation, of the mechanical chatter, it seems that we talk, but we don't really dialogue. We talk, but we do not go deep into any of our conversations. Conversations become boring and superficial because we avoid the unspoken and the silence that could open us up to real listening. However there is no room for silence between our islands. There is no more sea. There is sound garbage hiding the water, like floating objects to the shores of the island. There is too much noise, things and talk between us, and dialogue becomes impossible.

Besides, there is an even more complicated moment. It is about being able to talk to someone who is not willing to understand anything about it. It is about seeking dialogue in the scenario of this powerlessness. This is representative of the general unavailability of understanding in the midst of so much linguistic and technological waste.

The inability to understand results means a lack of openness to the other. This lack of openness, which in everyday life is the simple impotence for dialogue, is easily transmuted into denial of the other, hatred of the other, discourses and practices of humiliation, symbolic and physical violence, and, in the extreme, goes to the extermination of the other. We would have to find the mystery of the other. This mystery would be expressed as ethical availability.

Fear is the deep core of self-preservation and, in the extreme, of conservatism as a practice of denial. Listening, which is often a much more complex attitude than talking, is out of the question when we are afraid. The other enters our island when we hear him and destabilizes us. It is as if the other always demanded too much of us: the other threatens our certainties, and also our doubts, the other puts us in cognitive and affective check, that is, threatens us in relation to what we know and feel. Listening to them can be unbearable, but not just because they are different. It is possible that, like us, the other is also isolated and does not stop speaking in clichés and this moves us further and further away. We get into a vicious circle of denial.

We can exchange the metaphor of the island for the metaphor of the mirror. The other can be an opaque mirror of ourselves, as unwanted as we are to ourselves. Because there is narcissism in the midst of this inability to reach the other. There is no guarantee of self-respect in narcissism, only of the illusion that someone, even if it is only for myself, has become an image to be contemplated. We prefer to live in the mirror, because it is clear that the real that is beyond it bothers us even more than our transformation into an image.

The gesture of listening to those sounds requires effort. Now, every intelligent gesture is, in the first place, that of an effort. That gesture is like riding a bike. You have a time when it happens, but only if, we also want it enough, that we insist on it until we achieve it.

Hence, it is not just a matter of effort but of desire. It is not only a will but also a deep inclination whose sources would not be easy to identify since what we call desire does not seem to belong to language. However it does and it constitutes it. It may seem that it exists before us and yet it is in our mysterious genesis. The desire to listen to the other would be in us. Still, it disappears from our lives easily; leaving a trail of mystery that can only be explained by the fear of the other. It is fear of that someone we can only see as if they were nobody.

BIBLIOGRAPHY

Adorno, Theodor; Horkheimer, Max. *Dialética do Esclarecimento*. Rio de Janeiro: Zahar, 1984.

Adorno, Theodor; Horkheimer, Max. *Dialektik der Aufklärung. Philosophische Fragmente*. In: Adorno, Theodor Wisengrund. *Gesammelte Werke*, Vol. 3. Frankfurt am Main: Suhrkamp, 1997.

Adorno, Theodor; Frenkel-Brunswik, Else; Levinson, Daniel; Sanford, Nevitt. *The Authoritarian Personality*. London and New York: Verso, 2019.

Adorno, Theodor. "Education After Auschwitz," *Critical Models: Interventions and Catchwords*, trans. Henry W. Pickford. New York: Columbia University Press, 2005.

Adorno, Theodor. *Aspekte des neuen Rechts-Radikalismus*. Berlin: Suhrkamp, 2019.

Adorno, Theodor. *Die Freudische Theorie und die Struktur der fascistichen Propaganda*. Gesammelte Schriften Vol. 8, T. I [Soziologische Schriften]: Surhkamp Verlag, 1975, pp. 408–33.

Adorno, Theodor. *Stichworte: Kritische Modelle II*. Frankfurt am Main: Suhrkamp, 1969.

Adorno, Theodor. *Theorie der Halbbildung*. In A. Busch (Hrsg.), Soziologie und moderne Gesellschaft: Verhandlungen des 14. Deutschen Soziologentages vom 20. bis 24. Mai 1959 in Berlin (S. 169–191). Stuttgart: Ferdinand Enke. https://nbn-resolving.org/urn:nbn:de:0168-ssoar-160841

Agamben, Giorgio. *Homo Sacer. Il Potere Sovrano e la nuda vita*. Torino: Einaudi, 2004.

Agamben, Giorgio. *O que é o contemporâneo e outros ensaios*. Trans. Vinicius Honesko. Chapecó/ SC: Argos, 2009.

Arendt, Hannah. *Eichmann in Jerusalem*. Penguin, 2006.

Atwood, Margaret. *The Handmaid's Tale*. Boston: Houghton Mifflin Harcourt, 1986.

Austin, J.L. *How to Do Things with Words*, 2nd edn, M. Sbisà and J.O. Urmson (eds), Oxford: Oxford University Press, 1975.

Bandeira, Luiz Alberto Moniz. "As políticas neoliberais e a crise na América do Sul." Revista brasileira de Política Internacional, *Brasília*, Vol. 45, No. 2, pp. 135–46, December, 2002.

Barthes, Roland. *Comment vivre ensemble: Courses and seminars at the Collège de France (1976–1977)*, Seuil, 2002.

Benjamin, Walter. Kapitalismus als Religion. [Fragment]. In: *Gesammelte Schriften*, Hrsg.: Rolf Tiedemann und Hermann Schweppenhäuser, 7 Bde, Frankfurt am Main: Suhrkamp, 1. Auflage, 1991, Bd. VI, S. 100–2.

Benjamin, Walter. *The Storyteller Essays*. New York Review Books Classics, 2019.

Benjamin, Walter. *Über den Begriff der Geschichte*. Berlin: Suhrkamp, 2010.

Benjamin, Walter. *Work of Art in the Age of Its Technological Reproducibility, and Other Writings on Media*. Harvard University Press, 2008.

Bhabha, Homi. *The location of culture*. London: Routledge, 2004.

Bloch, R. Howard. *Medieval Misogyny and the Invention of Western Romantic Love*. Chicago: University of Chicago Press, 1992.

Bourdieu, Pierre. *Outline of a theory of practice*. Cambridge University Press, 1977.

Bourdieu, Pierre. *Le Sens Pratique*, Paris: Édition De Minuit, 1980.

Butler, Judith. *Gender Trouble: Feminism and the Subversion of Identity*. London: Routledge, 1990.

Caillois, Roger. *Les jeus et les hommes. Le masque et le Vertige*. Gallimard, 1967.

Campos, Leonildo Silveira. *Teatro, templo e mercado : organização e marketing de um empreendimento neopentecostal*. São Paulo: editora Vozes, 1997.

Canetti, Elias. *Mass and Power [Masse und macht]*. Farrar, Straus and Giroux, 1984.

Casara, Rubens. *Estado Pós-Democrático. Neo-obscurantismo e gestão dos indesejáveis*. Rio de Janeiro: Civilização Brasileira, 2017.

Casara, Rubens. *Sociedade sem lei: Pós-democracia, personalidade autoritária, idiotização e barbárie*. Rio de Janeiro: Civilização Brasileira, 2018.

Colón, Cristóbal. *Relaciones y Cartas de Cristóbal Colón*. Madrid: Libreria de la viuda de Hernando Y.C., 1892.

Cusicanqui, Silvia Rivera. *Ch'ixinakax utxiwa : una reflexión sobre prácticas y discursos descolonizadores*. 1st edn. Buenos Aires : Tinta Limón, 2010.

Debord, Guy. *La Societé du Spectacle*. Paris: Gallimard, 1996.

Descartes, René. Discours de la Méthode. In: *Œuvres complètes, III: Discours de la Méthode/Dioptrique/Météores/La Géométrie*. Paris: Gallimard, 2009.

Duby, Georges. *Dames du XIIe Siécle*. Paris: Gallimard, 1995.

Eco, Umberto. *Il fascismo eterno. La nave di Teseo*, 2017.

Federici, Silvia. *Caliban and the Witch*. Milano: Autonomedia, 2004.

Flusser, Vilém. *Filosofia da caixa preta*. Rio de Janeiro: Relume Dumará, 2002.

Foucault, Michel. *A microfísica do Poder*. Rio de Janeiro: Paz e Terra, 2000.

Foucault, Michel. *Histoire de la Sexualité*. La Volonté de Savoir. Paris, Gallimard, 1994.

Foucault, Michel. *Il faut défendre la société*. Cours au Collège de France. Paris: 1975. Ehhess, Gallimard, Seuil, 1976.

Foucault, Michel. *Le Courage de la vérité. Le Gouvernement de soi et des autres*. Paris: Ehhess, Gallimard, Seuil, 1984.

Foucault, Michel. *Les Anormaux. Cours au Collège de France, 1974–1975*. Paris: Ehhess, Gallimard, Seuil, 1999.

Frankfurt, Harry. *On Truth*. New York: Alfred A. Knopf, 2006.

Freud, Sigmund. "Psychoanalytische Bemerkungen über einen autobiographisch beschriebenen Fall von Paranoia (Dementia paranoides)." *Gesammelte Werke, Bd. 8, Werke aus den Jahren 1909–1913*. Frankfurt am Main, Fischer, 1998.

Freud, Sigmund. *Jenseits des Lustprinzips / Massenpsychologie und Ich-Analyse / Das Ich und das Es: Und andere Werke aus den Jahren 1920–1924*. Frankfurt am Main, Fischer, 1998.

Freud, Sigmund. *The Schreber Case*. London: Penguim, 2003.

Freud, Sigmund. *Totem und Tabu. Einige Übereinstimmungen im Seelenleben der Wilden und der Neurotiker*. Frankfut am Main: Fischer, 2013.

Freud, Sigmund. "Trauer und Melancholie." In: *Werke aus den Jahren 1913–1917*. Frankfurt am Main, Fischer, 2010.

Gonzales, Lélia; Hasenbalg, Carlos. *Lugar de negro*. Rio de Janeiro: Marco Zero, 1982.

Harvey, David. *The condition of postmodernity*. Oxford: Blackwell, 1989.

Holanda. Sérgio Buarque de. *Raízes do Brasil*. Rio de Janeiro: José Olympio, 1971.

Homer. *The Odyssey*, London: Penguin, 2009.

Ianni, Octavio. "Neoliberalismo e Nazi-fascismo." *Crítica Marxista*, São Paulo, Shaman, Vol. 1, No. 7, 1998, pp. 112–20.

Jason, Stanley. *How Fascism Works: The Politics of US and Them*. London: Random House, 2018.

Kafka, Franz. *Narrativas do espólio*. Trans. Modesto Carone. São Paulo: Companhia das Letras, 2002.

Klein, Melanie. *Envy and Gratitude and other works 1946–1963*. Vintage Classics, 1996.

Klein, Naomi. *The Shock Doctrine: The Rise of Disaster Capitalism*. London: Picador, 2008.

Laclau, Ernesto. *Emancipação e Diferença*. Rio de Janeiro : Eduerj, 2011.

Lévi-Strauss, C. *Tristes tropiques*. Paris, Plon, 1955.

Longerich, Peter. *Goebbels: a Biography*. London: Random House, 2015.

Maris, Bernard and Dostaller, Gilles. *Capitalisme et Pulsion de Mort*. Paris: Albin Michel, 2009.

Mbembe, Achille. *Políticas da Inimizade*. Trans. Maria Lança. Lisboa: Antígona, 2017.

Mbembe, Achille. *Critique de la raison nègre*. Paris: La Découverte, 2013.

Memmi, Albert. *Portrait du colonisé precedé de portrait du colonisateur*. Paris: Gallimard, 1957.

Mészáros, István. *A Educação para Além do Capital*. Trans. Isa Tavares. São Paulo: Boitempo Editorial, 2005.

Musil, Robert. *Da estupidez*. Trans. Manuel Alberto. Lisbon: Relógio D'Água, 1994.

Nancy, Jean-Luc and Lacoue-Labarthe, Philippe. *Le mythe nazi*: Paris: De L'Aube, 2016.

Nietzsche, Friedrich. *Also sprach Zarathustra/Thus Spoke Zarathustra*: German/English Bilingual Text. JiaHu Books, 2013.

Nietzsche, Friedrich. *Die Fröliche Wissenchaft*. München: Carl Hanser, 1994.

Nietzsche, Friedrich. *Über Warheit und Lüge im aussermoralischen Sinn. Werke in drei Bänden*. München: Carl Hanser, 1973.

190   BIBLIOGRAPHY

Oliveira Júnior, Rimabar José. "Capitalismo Gore no Brasil: entre farmacopornografia e necropolítica, o golden shower e a continência de Bolsonaro." *Revista Sociologias Plurais*, Vol. 5, No. 1, pp. 245–72, July, 2019.

Paxton, Robert Owe. *Anatomy of Fascism*. London: Penguin: 2004.

Said, Edward W. *Orientalismo: o Oriente como invenção do Ocidente*. Trans. Rosaura Eichemberg. São Paulo: Companhia das Letras, 2007.

Said, Flavia. "Ex-aliados de Bolsonaro mostram como funciona o Gabinete do Ódio." *Congresso em Foco*, Brasília, May 28, 2020. Available at: www.congressoemfoco.uol.com.br/governo/ex-aliados-de-bolsonaro-detalham-modus-operandi-do-gabinete-do-odio/

Sayak, Valencia Triana. "Capitalismo *gore* y necropolítica en México contemporâneo" [*Gore* and necropolitical capitalism in contemporary Mexico]. Relaciones Internacionales, No. 19, February 2012. GERI - UAM.

Schopenhauer, Arthur. *The Two Fundamental Problems of Ethics*. Cambridge University Press, 2009.

Tarde, 2 Gabriel. *La opinion et la foule*. CreateSpace Independent Publishing Platform, 2016.

Tiburi, Marcia. *Complexo de Vita-Lata: análise da humilhação colonial brasileira (Mongrel complex: analysis of the Brazilian colonial humiliation)*. Rio de Janeiro: Record, 2021.

Tiburi, Marcia. *Delírio do Poder – Psicopoder e Loucura coletiva na era da desinformação*. Rio de Janeiro: Record, 2019.

Tiburi, Marcia. *Filosofia em comum (Philosophy in common)*, Rio de Janeiro: Record, 2008.

Tiburi, Marcia. *Olho de Vidro. A televisão e o estado de exceção da imagem [Glass eye: the television and the state of exception of the image]*. Rio de Janeiro: Record, 2011.

Tiburi, Marcia. *Ridículo Político. O risível, manipulação da imagem e o esteticamente correto [Political ridiculous. The laughable, image manipulation and the aesthetically correct]*. Rio de Janeiro: Record, 2017.

Tiburi, Marcia. "The Functionality of Gender Ideology in the Brazilian Political and Economics Context." In: Foley, Conor. *In Spite of You: Bolsonaro and the New Brazilian Resistance*. New York and London: OR Books, 2018.

Todorov, Tzvetan. *The conquest of America the question of the other*. Translated from the french by Richard Howard. London: Harper Colophon Books, 1984.

Tolstoy, Leo. *Death of Ivan Ilitch*. Penguin, 2016.

Türcke, Christoph. *Sociedade Excitada: Filosofia da Sensação [Excited society: Philosophy of sensation]*. Campinas: Unicamp, 2010.

Viveiros De Castro, Eduardo. *A inconstância da alma selvagem*. São Paulo: Cosacnaify, 2006.

Wittgenstein, Ludwig. *Philosophische Untersuchungen*. Frankfurt am Main Suhrkamp, 2003.

INDEX